THE SUBVERSION AGAINST THE UNITED STATES

By

Ed Prida II & Edward Prida III

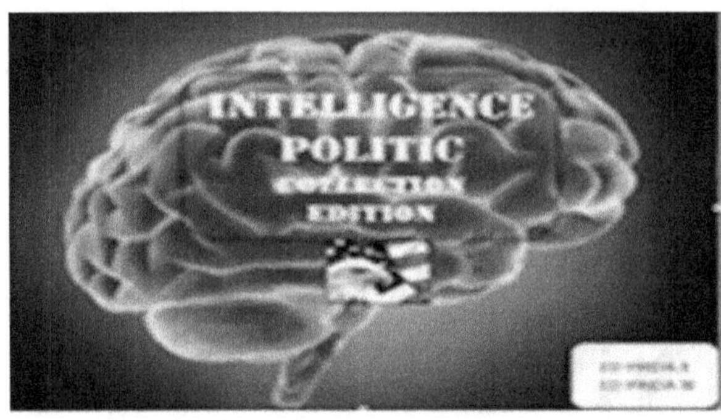

This book is part of "La Sovietización de Cuba y sus Consecuencias"

English version of "La Subversion contra Estados Unidos y Cuba" (Spanish)

Dedicatory:

In Memory of my Masters Colonel KGB Victor Pina and, Yuri Besmenov, Rolando Barros and General Jose Abrantes, for ever thankful, they gave me the True. In special Abrantes encarceleated and assasinated had the Master Plan to finish with the Castro's regime, Castro won because he had deep spies net in the United States. How the Soviets had been catched and destroying our countries (United States and Cuba) and Humankind.

Prof. Ed Prida

Thankfully, to my few friends who help me with emotional support. To my enemies who get me the reasons to do it..

Ed Prida II

TABLE OF CONTENTS

Chapter # 1

Subversion: The Political, Ideological, and Legal Definition

Introduction

Many times, in our life, we listen about this theme but a few times we search for the meaning of this unusual word. The concept of subversion is ancient; they used it in China, back in the fourth century BC, by a general and philosopher named Sun Tse.

Since that time this has been the way to win a war without a battlefield.

In the Dictionary of the British Oxford University, the word subversion makes its entry, in the late Middle Ages, to the English language from the French subvert; and this Latin "subvertere" sub compound prefix and suffix below vertere mean change. The Larousse dictionary defines it as: "an action against established values." For intelligence agencies, subversion is a style of war tactics that distracts attention from the real target and from those who execute it because it is done within a framework of acceptable legal action using the most civilized channels of relations between the different factors that make up a country including diplomatic and academic relations between the different countries, especially for countries with totalitarian models, these two categories are absolutely used according to Intelligence and Subversion.

Operational Concept

There are many operational definitions of the concept of Subversion, and all make it easier to understand its essence.

The subversion is a process to be described as an attack on the public morale and, "the will to resist interventions are the products of combined political and social loyalties they usually attach which to national symbols. Disintegration of political and social institutions of the state, these loyalties may be detached and transferred to the political or ideological cause of the aggressor.

 They use Subversion as a tool to achieve political goals because it carries less risk, cost, but much more time and difficulty as opposed to open belligerency.

Like clear advantage, it is a relatively cheap form of warfare that does not require large amounts of training and weapons. A subversive is something or someone carries the potential for some degree of socio-political damage. In this context, they sometimes call a "subversive" a "traitor" concerning (and usually by) the government in power.

The Subversion: Operative Definitions

Some concepts may make it easier to understand because the word "Subversion" has a wide use, probably the problem with defining the term subversion is that there is not a single definition that is accepted.

Charles Townshend described subversion as a term, "so elastic as to be virtually devoid of meaning, and its use does little more than convey the enlarged sense of the vulnerability of modern systems to all kinds of covert assaults".

"Subversion is the undermining or detachment of the loyalties of significant political and social groups within the victimized state, and their transference, under ideal conditions, to the symbols and institutions of the aggressor. "Subversion — Actions designed to undermine the military, economic, psychological, or political strength or morale, of a governing authority.

Legal Concept

"Subversive Action. Anyone lends aid, comfort, and moral support individuals, groups, or organizations that advocate the overthrow of incumbent governments by force and violence is subversive and is engaged in subversive activity. They will place all willful acts that are intended to be detrimental to the best interests of the government and that do not fall into the categories of treason, sedition, sabotage, or espionage in the category of subversive activity."

"Subversive Political Action — A planned series of activities designed to accomplish political objectives by influencing, dominating, or displacing individuals or groups who are so placed as to affect the decisions and actions of another government."

Subversion — "A destructive, aggressive activity aimed to destroy the country, nation, or geographical area of your enemy... [By demoralizing the cultural values and changing the population's perception of reality].

Subversion — This is part of the Psychological War using public media, under legal action, as being blocking different type of actions, as political, economic, psychological and military that aims at the overthrow of established new authority in a country."

https://www.jstor.org/stable/1409771?seq=1#page_scan_tab_contents

Conceptual understanding of subversion

Defining and understanding subversion means identifying entities, structures, and things that can be subverted. It may help to identify practices and tools that are not subversive. I can subvert institutions and morals, but ideology cannot.

The fall of a government, or the creation of a new government because of an external war is not subversion. Espionage does not count as subversion directly because it is not an action that leads directly to the overthrow of a government. Information gathered from espionage may plan and carry out subversive activities. To gain an understanding of what is subversive requires understanding the intent of those acting. This makes defining and identifying subversion a difficult process.

The totalitarian regime does not allow the critic because, because the criticism can do damage and help the opposition to overthrow the tyranny. Still when to criticize a power with the intention to reform government or to change its policies is not a subversive behavior, even though too much critics by different source   may contribute to an overthrow. But criticism intended to help a planned   overthrow becomes subversive without regard to whether it is right or wrong."

 The "Fake News" is the Voluntary Subversive Role

Subversion, however, is also often a goal of "dummies", artists and people in those careers. Here, being subversive can mean questioning, poking fun at, and undermining the established order.

The humoristic is referred to as being subversive, it is as much of a compliment to their work as it could be an accusation, from comics scene manipulate critic or point of view to serve the subversive campaign in long term. These group are prominent and intensive developer of the communists and anti-American ideas.

Irony is one of the most potent forms of subversion in the Scenic Art. They can touch deep in our mind. The Media are the main resource of Subversion that can be voluntary or by purchase.

 Types of subversion

They can break the Subversion down into internal and external subversion. This does not mean that each type of subversion follows a specific playbook using predetermined tools and practices.

Each subversive campaign is different because of the social, political, economic, cultural, and historical differences that each country has.

They use subversive activities based on an evaluation of these factors. This breakdown merely clarifies who the actors are. While the subversive actors may be different, the soon to be subverted targets are the same.

The foreing forces and interest came from another country what has an interest to attack or destroy the opponent. These actions taken by another country in cooperation with a native who got a deep washing brain and after represent the enemy, the target is subverted country and can a tool of statecraft. Foreign agents from another country are not efficient to work like external subversion or work in clandestine status. The observers or the country population can suspect that the activity has some relation with exterior, but nobody has proof of it.

The reason for this is the individuals that may legitimately share the cause of the internal subversive dissidents and legitimately have volunteered. Only when the government itself furnishes a nation with money, arms, supplies, or other help to dissidents can it be called external subversion.

<u>Better Social Environment to Apply the Political Subversion</u>

Unfortunately, the more rights and freedoms they have in a country, they can subvert the more.

Democracies that guarantee rights higher than they can offer become very weak and vulnerable to subversive attacks that are invisible and silent.

It would be practically impossible to penetrate a closed and totalitarian society because the media are under the control of dictatorships, as of Russia, China, Cuba, North Korea, Venezuela, etc. Other countries that, although they do not have a totalitarian and centralized regime when they have a cultural heritage as well internalized, can also be invulnerable to subversive processes, such as Japan India and the Arab world for its ancient religion. In both types of countries, totalitarians and closed culture, foreign propaganda always has a destination: go to the garbage and be consumed by fire; they prohibit even letters from individual to an individual so that the person does not receive information contrary to the official.

At present, espionage, as we see in novels and films, specifically focused on finding certain information, occupies 10 to 15% of the economic resources and working time of the intelligence agencies of totalitarian countries; While <u>subversion consumes 85%</u> of the rest of the general intelligence activity.

Within this activity, there is the work of ideological penetration that can, without using nuclear missiles, subvert or change the profiles of a government in favor of the communists.

This method has been successful in Rhodesia, Vietnam, Bangladesh, Cuba, Nicaragua, Angola, Venezuela, Bolivia, Ecuador, Chile, Argentina, Iraq, Ethiopia, North Yemen, Iran, the United States, and others.

The arsenal of Psychological Warfare of the USSR is top secret and perfidious tool get countries. I learned directly from my mentor Colonel KGB Victor Pina Cardoso, Captain Julian Garcia Oliva, MD and by the book from Yuri Bezmenov, at last, then I understood in deep the scope of this military specialty mixed with Social Psychology and how they drove the political, cultural and military issues to get the Republic of Cuba to be like a military base against the United States.

As well as other techniques like the Cognitive Dissonance created by Leon Festinger, to create the modification of attitudes that the American pilots underwent when they were prisoners in North Viet Nan taken secretly to Cuba to be subjected to special kind of torture to create contradictions to them when they were returned to the United States. Many of them have erratic thinking and behavior after they returned in freedom to the USA when the War ended.

All this information gives us an explanation of how many events occurred; the Soviets have gone unnoticed as the true authors of the same.

Detect Subversion

Subversion must be identified to neutralize it. It is necessary to recognize the entities, structures and their induced cessation that have an origin and resources undetectable but capable of creating crisis and lack of control over a nation, to create the total collapse. However, if we ask ourselves what and for whom it serves what has happened, we have a response from those who orchestrated the event.

It is very important to identify the mechanisms and induced events used by the enemy that by their appearance are not subversive. Institutions and morality can be subverted to erase ideological values.

<u>The "false news" plays a fundamental support role for voluntary subversion</u>.

Subversion, however, it is also often a goal of "Fools" artists and people in those professions that have access to many people, considering themselves as opinion leaders or emerging. Here, being subversive can mean questioning, mocking and undermining the established order. When talking about comedy or subversive humor, it is a message as effective as a denunciation can be? The media is the main war equipment of the Subversion, it can be voluntary or by contract.

The Subversion Plan is for long time, between 15 or 20 years to get result. Each type of subversion follows a specific method using the conditions of where and when it is going to be used as well as the type of tools and practices used to depend on the objective. Subversive campaigns are designed according to the country or region where it will be applied due to the social, political, economic, cultural and historical differences that each country has.

They use subversive activities based on an evaluation of these factors. In the first place, it is necessary to locate which is the most important aim, where to focus to "clean the brain" of the average individual, this breakdown simply clarifies who the actors are.   Although the subversive actors may be different, the subverted objectives are the same.

The layers or governing structures and policies are the ultimate goals of persuasion because they control the physical instruments of state power and the goal of subversion is to make them lose control.

The subversion comes from another country in cooperation with the internal forces and later it becomes an efficient tool to control. Foreign volunteers from another country can cooperate to introduce and implement external subversion usually by financial support and advice.

The reason for this is individuals who can legitimately share the cause of subversive internal dissidents and have legitimately volunteered. Only when the government itself provides a nation with money, weapons, supplies or other aid to dissidents can it be called external subversion.

Optimal terrain for political subversion

Unfortunately, the more rights and freedoms there are in a country, the easier it is to accept subversion.

For this reason, representative democracies that guarantee citizenship rights beyond what they can economically offer become very weak and vulnerable to subversive attacks, making them generalized to all levels of the population, invisible and silent. This is one of the ways in which liberals are used to sustain the destructive maneuver of the massive invasion of immigrants, the vast majority unproductive mass that consumes much of the social resources produced by nationals and destined to these, and resources that are diverted to people who are not entitled to them.

On the contrary, it is practically impossible to use these subversive mechanisms and penetrate a closed and totalitarian society because the mass media are under the control of dictatorships, as is the case of Russia, China, Cuba, North Korea, Venezuela, etc.

Other countries that, although they do not have a totalitarian and centralized regime when they have a cultural heritage well internalized in the social conscience, become invulnerable to subversive processes, as we can see Japan, India and the Arab world by its ancient religion. In both types of countries, totalitarian and with a closed culture, foreign propaganda always has a destiny: to go to the garbage and be consumed by fire; In totalitarian systems it is known practice interception of communication whether written or digital will be subject to the supervision of specialists to detect any information that contradicts the official information of the regime on any event or event.

Within this activity, there is the work of ideological penetration that can, without using nuclear missiles, subvert or change the profiles of a government in favor of the communists.

This method has been successful in Rhodesia, Vietnam, Bangladesh, Cuba, Nicaragua, Angola, Venezuela, Bolivia, Ecuador, Chile, Argentina, Iraq, Ethiopia, North Yemen, Iran, the United States, and others.

The arsenal of the Psychological War of the USSR is the most secret and treacherous weaponry ever used.   The bitter lessons of Soviet subversion in Cuba by the Caribbean group of the KGB and its leader with the pseudonym of the Caribbean Fox, Fabio Grobart (Juan Blanco), Josh Cohen, and his main operative Víctor Pina Cardoso and the General of the KGB Nikolai Leonov.

Political and Ideological Subversion is the application of the tools and scientific concepts of Social Psychology, the Classic Psychology using data from Forensic Science, Laws, Demography, Sociology and the directed use of mass media.

The KGB and GRU, and other related political groups that prepare emerging leaders and penetration agents to supposedly create images of others, independent and contrary to the well-known Communist Parties, these "leaders" apply all kinds of techniques to be controlled docilely and produce automatic behaviors by hypnotic induction or under drugs. Which can induce certain people to make attacks, sabotage, etc., these are classic applications of Military Psychology?

The Cognitive Dissonance created by Leon Festinger was used by Cuba against US military pilots imprisoned in North Vietnam and later a selected group were taken secretly to Cuba. There they were subjected to tasks and stimuli for emotional imbalance, hunger, thirst, physical pain, harassment, loss of the notion of time, absence of sun, isolation, differential treatment, etc. This method deactivates interpersonal relationships within the group so that everyone feels isolated and betrayed by the rest of the group, cognitively applied stimuli to create conflicts with attitudes opposed to their original convictions and erratic behaviors capable of developing and projecting when they were returned to the United States.

The purpose of this procedure was to demoralize the Armed Forces of the United States and their efforts to stop the invasion of the North over the South.

There are other types of symptoms in some prisoners known in the post-war Clinical Psychiatry as Stockholm Syndrome. There may be some difference between the two methods; those who gain the Stockholm syndrome voluntarily identify themselves with their punishers or captors without a psychological procedure having conditioned such affiliations with their enemies. The method followed by the totalitarian countries is different, they use supra stimuli, such as isolation, loss of orientation in time and space, hunger and mistreatment, beatings, lack of hygiene and medical care, the typical example were the American pilots captured in Vietnam, subjected to a regime of psychological and physical torture systematically to subject them to the method of "Cognitive Dissonance" method that pursues the change of "attitude" of the individual and we have seen how some of them persist the lack of coherence in their attitudes .

Cognitive Dissonance

Each person has a strong inner need for their attitudes and behavior is coherent and balanced among them. When an inconsistency is introduced, the mind search for an element that produces a lack of harmony, which produces internal tension, but the search will continue until it is resolved.

The discomfort, stress or anxiety experienced by individuals when their beliefs or attitudes conflict with what they do. This displeasure can lead to behavior change or renounce their attitudes through lying himself when *fail to get benefits needed.*

True or false

When there is little extrinsic motivation in a person to justify a behavior that goes against his attitude, then he changes his mind to rationalize our actions.

The results of an experiment by Festinger illustrate the importance of the use of monotonous and difficult tasks used on prisoners or citizens of totalitarian countries like Voluntary Job.

Three groups to perform a task or no assessed as boring were used.

 Later, he was asked subjects to lie, because they had to tell a new group that would continue the same task, it was fun. Group 1 could leave without saying anything to the new group, group 2 was paid 1 dollar before lying and group 3 was paid 20 dollars.

A week later, Festinger called the subjects of the study to ask what they thought of the task. Group 1 and 3 answered that the task was boring, while group 2 had replied that he s funny like that. Why did the members of the group who had received only 1 dollar claim that the task had been fun?

The researchers concluded that people experience a dissonance between conflicting cognitions. When receiving only 1 dollar, students were forced to change their thinking, because they had no other justification (1 dollar was insufficient and produced cognitive dissonance). Those who had received $ 20, however, had external justification for their behavior and therefore experienced less dissonance. This seems to indicate that if there is no external cause that justifies the behavior, it is easier to change beliefs or attitudes.

 When cognitive dissonance occurs, in addition to making active attempts to reduce it, the individual usually avoids conflict situations. At a social level, cognitive dissonance is used within the design of operations of political and ideological subversion.

The FBI found that a sample of 1200 abductees only 8% identified with their captors and this hard a relatively short time.

The Stockholm's Syndrome is a change of attitude and behavior by a defense mechanism that forms an effective bond of dependence and justifies its captors, in a way that is changing their attitudes to take the same attitude as their captors, assuming their behavior styles, ideas, motivations, beliefs or reasons used by the kidnappers to deprive them of freedom. They also know him as the "Survival Identification Syndrome". When the victim is released, he can present samples that show he suffers from the syndrome because he always tries to look like his captors.

These principles endorsed by experiments explain how people from totalitarian systems in their vast majority in some way maintain a nexus of identification with the abuse and absence of human rights suffered. They try to justify and accept the injustice they received, we arrive at the sad conclusion that they adapted to live in captivity, precisely this is what globalism, communism and all forms of oppression pursue.

All this information it gives us a frame of reference to reevaluate the enemies and analyze many events that have occurred with a spontaneous appearance and many blame the CIA; the Soviets have gone unnoticed as the authors of these attacks. The Russians are heirs and followers of these techniques and have seen the success in politics. We are seeing new ways they demoralize and leave all potentials out of the political scene. They are effective to create "sources of rumor" writing opinions in large quantities and confusing the public opinion creating conflicts, deceptions and divisionism.

Subversion Categories

• Create façade groups and manipulate existing political parties, examples: Liberal people as Republican Candidate supported by the enemy.

• Infiltration of the armed forces, police and other state institutions, as well as important non-governmental organizations.

• Generate civil disturbances through strikes and boycott.

• The creation of new organizations with the order of the day, but with different names but in secret leadership, but everybody under the control of communists.

"The ideas are more powerful than weapons.   We do not want enemies to have weapons.   Why should we let them have ideas?   Joseph Stalin

"The victim's position is powerful.   The victim is always morally correct, not responsible, and always has the right to sympathy. " Dr. Offer Zur, Psychology of Victimology

"The Western world has been completely saturated with Christianity for 2000 years ... any country based on Judeo-Christian values cannot, therefore, be overthrown until those roots are cut ... but to cut the roots, to change the culture, a Long March through the institutions is necessary. Only then the energy will fall in our laps like ripe fruit! " Antonio Gramsci

Ref.

1.   Auerbach, S., Kiesler, D., Stentz, T., Schmidt, J., Devany Serio, C. (1994). Interpersonal and adjustment to the stress of simulated captivity: an empirical test of the Stockholm Syndrome. *Journal of Social and Clinical Psychology, 13 (2), 207-221.*

2.   Vállus, C. (2002). About the Stockholm Syndrome. *Medicine Clinic*, 119 (5).

3.   Carver, JM Love and Stockholm syndrome: the mystery of loving an abuser. Taken from: cepvi.com.

4.   Domen, ML (2005). An "incomprehensible" link between its protagonists: The Stockholm Syndrome. *Encrucijadas, 33, University of Buenos Aires.*

5.   Graham, D. Et al. (nineteen ninety-five). A Scale for Identifying "Stockholm Syndrome". Reactions in Young Dating Women: Factor Structure, Reliability, and Validity. *Violence and Victims, 10 (1).*

6.   Montero, A. The syndrome of domestic Stockholm in battered women. *Spanish Society of Psychology of Violence.*

7.   Montero Gómez, A. (1999). Psychopathology of the Stockholm Syndrome: Essay of an etiological model. *Science Police, 51*

8.   Muñoz Endre, J. (2008). Femicide. *Estudios Policiales Magazine, 3.*

9.   Parker, M. (2006). Stockholm Syndrome *Management Learning, 37 (1), 39-41*

10.   He *Diagnostic and Statistical Manual of Mental Disorders (DSM-5)* of the American Psychiatric Association.

11.   The *International Classification of Diseases (ICD-10)* of the World Health Organization

12. Cognitive Dissonance Theory |
https://www.simplypsychology.org/cognitive-dissonance.html

13, Festinger's (1957) cognitive dissonance theory suggests that we have an inner ...[PDF] psychologist Leon Festinger developed the cognitive dissonance theory (Festinger, 1957). The theory has obviously stood the ...

14.Cognitive dissonance – Wikipedia https://en.wikipedia.org/wiki/Cognitive_dissonance

15.Disonancia cognitiva - WikiVisually
https://wikivisually.com/lang-es/wiki/Disonancia_cognitiva
-

16.Disonancia Cognitiva - Scribd
https://www.scribd.com/document/.../Disonancia-Cognitiva

https://www.jstor.org/stable/1409771?seq=1#page_scan_tab_contents

Chapter # 2

"The Frankfort School"

The first Subversion Plan against America started 1938. The Soviet Union dispatched many agents of the KGB, Jews and Communits. They arrived few time before the Second World War from Germany and from France and England, like a midway to get the United State.

The American leftist movement was very receptive to Marxist theories and openly criticized our society. They kept silent about the violation of Human Rights and all the monstrous atrocities of Lenin, Mao Tse Dong, Stalin, against their countries and the rest of the world.

The so-called Frankfurt School was an excellent "Trojan Horse" to infest with Marxist concept the American Way of Life. They introduced ideas to education, laws, arts, religion, labor class, armed forces, congress, senate, diplomatic services, all levels were gaining ground and today are already an impregnable bastion of Marxism in the Local Government, School Boards around the country, and very powerful in the like the Universities of Berkeley, George Washington, Brandeis and Princeton and in a way, we would say that throughout the United States´ education system and the American Way of Life, in many ways.

The new Trojan Horse is reborn in the thirties after a decade of daydreams; the Frankfurt School is heading towards a new goal, cleaning up the discredited Marxism and everything behind it as socialism, populism, the struggle of classes, gulag, etc.

Using the same procedure but changing the concepts and vocabulary because it was known that the negative influence of the Bolshevik Revolution, Lenin and Stalin had put in a difficult situation... since their acceptance as a social system, the people were not able to accept Marxism as a favorite system, especially in Europe.

The Frankfort School "ELEVEN POINTS PLAN"

.The undermining of schools 'and teachers' authority
.The creation of racism Offenses
.Continue change to create confusion
.The teaching of sex and homosexuality to children
.Huge immigration to destroy identity.
.The promotion of excessive drinking
.Emptying of churches
.An unreliable legal system with bias against perpe
trator of the crime
.Dependency on the state or state benefits
.Control and dumbing down of media
.Encouraging the breakdown of the family

 They were theorizing how to design a society, easy to keep in control at all levels, but when the group came to the United States, they started to introduce his ideas in Universities and Service Centers like Psychologists and Political Philosophies. They were trying to do a Social Engineering, a new concept to organize the society.

These new Marxists were looking for a way to revive Marx's ideas but with another appearance so that the "dynamic and important working class" could be manipulated without calling it a revolutionary class, it occurred to them to graft Karl Marx's dry tree with a blooming offspring of the libidinous concepts of the Austrian psychiatrist Sigmund Freud.

This new "fruit", created to poison the MAN of Western culture was the union of Sex and Politics, since according to Freud, the common man lived under constant psychological pressure according to the Freudian conceptual scheme of personality in its three instances : (The real self) and fundamentally obsessed with sex (impulses,named id) and frustrations created by social norms of coexistence (social discipline, superego or super me), this mixture is attributed to a Jew and Communists called Mark Horkheimer, Theodor Adorno and the neo-psychoanalyst Erich Fromm, who stated "the difference between male and female are not the aspects of essential sexual differences but are derived from differences in functions during life and that in large part have been established by society and not by nature", in other words, the fact, according them, these differences are purely artificial and so, everybody be homosexual is natural. As we see clearly, treating the natural or biological difference of sex is as absurd as "trying to cover the sun with a finger."

It does not seem necessary to delineate between functional, biological differences for all the instances of the differences in all species from masculine to feminine in all their functions. "In the praxis, the sex pleasure can be with the same sex plus imagination."

The team was joined by Herbert Marcuse and attributed to him to exalt sex as the central element of the so-called "Political Correction." It concept play the role of blinded forces in offensive.

This graft became, in fact, the theoretical basis of the American left, thanks to the fabulous welcome given to it by Columbia University, of New York City, led by Nicholas Murray Butler and induced by Julian Gumperz and Willi Muezemberg, both active and international communists, they had the political agenda hidden and as a result, we're watching it every day.

The KGB took good advantage of it with the before successful subversion job done by Frankfort School. As is known, although officially the powerful, Political and Ideological Subversion Operation, began with Yuri Andropov, Minister of the KGB in 1980 and launched from Cuba in May 1980, as you will read in the next chapters.

This new and aggressive plan against the United States was greatly favored by the psycho-social background of Jews German Marxist thinkers and psychologist refugees in the 1930s and 40s known by the "School of Frankfort of the Memo"but the real name was Institute of Social Research.

Psychologist members of the Frankfort School and their "Eleven Point" model, designed to destroy "Step by Step" the United States of America.

The Nazis came to power in Germany and the "Frankfurt School" members recognized that they were not safe (since they were Jewish and Marxist) - they all fled to US universities and continued their work. Due to the massive Jewish network within US academy, they all found top positions with ease.

The Eleven Point Plan

Karl Marx and Frederich Engels wrote "The Capital," with a critic point against the social and economic advance in England, France, and Germany around 1870-90. The practice of this theoretical approach just was executed in Russia, by the Bolshevik's starting in 1917 but after 15-20 years, Russia just got the internal civil war, misery, hunger, deaths, and prisoners. The impact of the Russian Revolution became a wrong reputation for the Marxists and Social Democracy Parties, especially in Europe.

But in Frankfort the Memo, a group of Philosophers and Psychologists with Marxist ideas, designed a Plan with a name, not to be identified with Marx's ideas and they concentrated the "great theory" in just Eleven Points.

They thought that to destroy any society, introduce those Eleven Points wisely, in silence, without protests, without a scandalous Revolution.

This Subversive Plan had hidden the true objective; only the communists knew what will be doing. These Eleven objectives have developed in theory, but nothing stands still, and much is hidden. So, think of these objectives in the context of the time they were created, and understand that some of them have massively developed as our World has changed.

In summary, we know of the so-called "Eleven Steps" that they contributed and that, generally, the noble and well-intentioned citizens of the United States, has not been conscious to interpret the reality of the causes and consequences of the social phenomenon that we are living in this last 60-70 years and now, we're in the swan .

The Silent Masses are working to fix our loved America.

It is not difficult to identify that all these objectives are living and creating a different kind of conflict against all social roles and status inside the American Society and also the Western culture. Today, the electronic advance gets the communication between each people fast, economic and easy. We can find that these are exactly the agenda that the Communist Party and his public branch the Democratic Party follow and they are red puppets.

When you read the following lines, you will understand what we are watching, we are living, and we are feeling the weight and the consequences of this Evil Plan, but the good news is that if you know it, you can defeat every single element of our enemies.

CHAPTER #3

Point One "Undermining of the School's and the Teacher Authority.

This point had a very special connotation and had been a transcendental transformation in the National School System. Every new generation of citizens continues receiving more and deeper brainwashing.

The Frankfort School "opens a new way" to resolve the "conflict between child and father". This new approach is given complete freedom to take decisions of the boy against the father, the children never accept the parent's mandatory styles, and the new wave is liberty for the children to take decisions without respect to the family rules, neither the school rules, neither society laws. Born as a new tendency, it does not respect the authority. Hollywood had been playing an evil role in this new destructive attitude in the new generations.

Margaret Mead, an American Psychologist and Social Anthropologist in this same time, caused an impact when she returned from Samoa Island with a really new

approach to the TeenAger Crisis, but the Frankfort School had more power and almost deleted Mead's approach.

. The School believed there were two types of revolution: (a) political and (b) cultural. Cultural Revolution demolishes from within. 'Modern forms of subjection are marked by mildness'. They saw it as a long-term project and kept their sights clearly focused on the family, education, media, sex and popular culture.

To make it shorter and more benign, the Frankfurt School opaques and shows us exactly the opposite, how to make the adolescent crisis more durable, dangerous, expensive and simply put, this was the strongest armament against the United States society in a very short term: Is to increase the symptoms and permanence of the psychological traits of the Adolescent Crisis indefinitely.

This crisis of personality is to some extent normal as a result of biological changes and the new role of the carrier at the level of his group and society.

 The Frankfort group malignantly caused this crisis and reinforced it by creating social conditions with sub-Social groups known as "victim groups" such as gays, blacks, immigrants, women, disabled people. Who have them in the spotlight by following the line of "politically correct" and themselves become identified automatically. The reverse clothing, winter clothes in the height of summer, extravagant hair colors, body make-up, tattoos, earrings and encrustations on the skin, atypical forms of walking, identification with enemy leaders and ideas. The idolatry to negative heroes, cults of death, and terror using human skulls, cadaver remain tortures, as emotional symbols, etc.

Also, the classic Psychology gave very important events in the process of the baby to understand and assimilate the meaning of the word NO, considering this step as the first behavior organizer.

The concept of NO, must be interiorized in the personality and can make the difference between the life or death in the first age, because it protect against the danger, but with time, the concept of no, became the main resource of adaptation inside the group where the children develop his life. The social inter action teach the limit of his personal liberty with the social laws.

It may be important to know the stages through which our psychological development transcends to obtain better results, applying the knowledge that has contributed many prestigious psychologists and epistemologists and that their excellent contributions have been validated by practice and logic, the psychologist Gordon W. Allport, a Harvard professor, others as Jean Piaget and Henri Wallon, both French psychologists, described how the development of moral concepts, their origin and how they are grafted to society in due course.

There may be many instances of personality that we could analyze, but I think the one that interests us most to understand its transcendence is the Moral Consciousness from the first age of the infant.

Consciousness is a whole, it can be passive, or it can be active, mobilizing or halting. It can be the perfect indicator of whom we are and where we are going. The development of the moral conscience has two moments in its formation; the first is the development and the second, its adult structure.

The first is directed towards obedience, the obligation to comply with rules or rules and adulthood becomes a duty, which if not done as it should, is a self-punishment, a sense of guilt and an uneasiness of conscience.

In his first stage a child at 18 months, his thinking has developed enough to encode and decrypt the sounds he receives, which are words, but the most commonly used word is the word NO, which means to limit his impulse, curb actions that are born from within as a biological or cognitive need or come from the perception of the external environment around him, which drives to explore and know.

He does not create a difference in his life and allows him to adapt and survive; he becomes the signifier of No, the main signifier of the organization of his being.

Shortly after they notice other signs, you have to, or you do not have to! These signs indicate subordination to rules established by the immediate authority and presage reward or punishment, which become reinforces of this or that behavior.

The reasons are still very complex for his thought, which does not allow comparing in different times like past, present and future, lives in the present with a small repertoire of the past, but there is no future dimension yet. This learning is not linear; it is tortuous as a spiral that sometimes ascends and at others descends. These rules begin to be fulfilled even in the absence of authority, and the acts are pure valued if it is fulfilled or not the regal, not important the circumstances.

 Little by little the right child becomes a moral realist, and the vulnerability of the rules cause frustration and anxiety, and this is a major compensation factor.

When children reach teenager level they consider that many of those rules were unreasonable and they're starting to break them, doing acts forbidden to demonstrate to himself his reason and power.

At the age of sixteen, he experiences new norms of conduct as trial and error, seeking justifications for his new reasoning that brings his evolution of analytical thinking. Gradually he is grafted into an adolescent of the conscience of duty, who has no external punishment and the supercar the concept of himself in development. In maturity, there is no fear of punishment, but an inner strength of the so-called "I have to." The moral conscience Mature guides towards an acceptable concept of itself and take the chosen course.

 But in all of this about history the very subtle but very powerful concept about how to teach the concept of NO were defeated and the Frankfurt School was the winner. Step by step the Education System was changed by the force of leftist or confused by the new ideas of our Legislative Branches at all levels.

The result is more and more new generation never keep in his mind to respect for the rules in the home after in the school and at last in the society.

There is a high probability that this kind of person becomes in honored members of the Non-Adaptable Army and longtime inmate in Psychiatric Hospital or Jails. Preventive action is required.

The increase of the <u>suicidal statistic, the inmates in prisons</u>, the unhappy peoples, the pessimist peoples and almost all of them a good candidate to be a member of the Democratic Party or good members of the Communist Party.

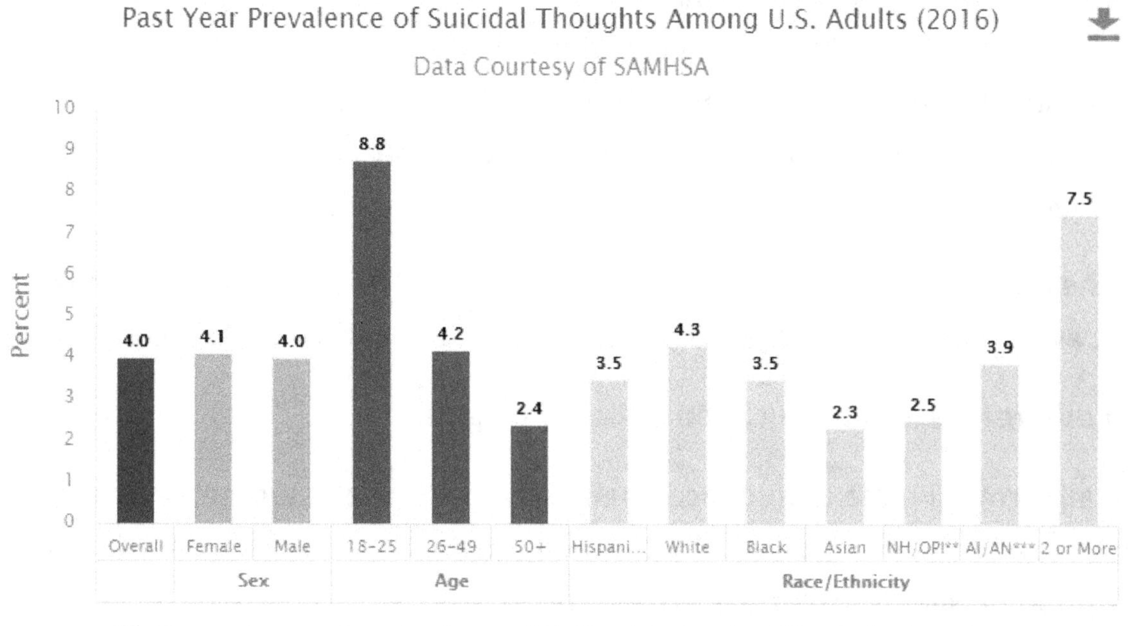

The suicidal is higher between 18-25 years old population.

	Leading Cause of Death in the United States (2016)				
	Data Courtesy of CDC				
			Select Age Groups		
Rank	**10-14**	**15-24**	**25-34**	**35-44**	**45-54**
1	Unintentional Injury 847	Unintentional Injury 13,895	Unintentional Injury 23,984	Unintentional Injury 20,975	Malignant Neoplasms 41,291
2	**Suicide 436**	**Suicide 5,723**	**Suicide 7,366**	Malignant Neoplasms 10,903	Heart Disease 34,027
3	Malignant Neoplasms 431	Homicide 5,172	Homicide 5,376	Heart Disease 10,477	Unintentional Injury 23,377
4	Homicide 147	Malignant Neoplasms 1,431	Malignant Neoplasms 3,791	**Suicide 7,030**	**Suicide 8,437**

The contribution factor, how to remark our society ideas of the Frankfurt School. The exploit Freud's idea of 'pan sexualize', this concept aim " the sex is anywhere, around you and inside you", the search for pleasure, the exploitation of the differences between the sexes, the overthrowing of traditional relationships between men and women. To further their aims they would:

• Attack the authority of the father, deny the specific roles of father and mother, and wrest away from families their rights as primary educators of their children.

• Abolish differences in the education of boys and girls

• Abolish all forms of male dominance - hence the presence of women in the armed forces, and the new police "No question, no answer" to increase discipline and corruption problems inside the Armed Forces.

• Declare women to be an 'oppressed class' and men as 'oppressors.'

ll International Socialist Movement, Chief of Propaganda Wily Munzenberg, left, summed up the Frankfurt School's long-term operation thus: 'We will make the West so corrupt that it stinks.' One of the results of the Subversion Plan is our prisoner population:

The countries with the highest prison population rate – the number of prisoners per 100,000 of the national population – the United States (698), St. Kitts & Nevis (607), Turkmenistan (583), U.S. Virgin Islands (542), Cuba (510), El Salvador (492), Guam - U.S.A. (469), Thailand (461), Belize (449), Russian Federation (445), Rwanda (434) and British Virgin Islands (425).

However, more than half of all countries and territories (55%) have a prison population rate of below 150 per 100,000.

The world prison population rate, based on United Nations estimates of national population levels, is 144 per 100,000.

http://www.prisonstudies.org/news/more-1035-million-people-are-prison-around-world-new-report-shows

The American criminal justice system holds more than 2.3 million people in 1,719 state prisons, 102 federal prisons, 2,259 juvenile correctional facilities, 3,283 local jails, and 79 Indian Country jails as well as in military prisons, immigration detention facilities, civil commitment centers, and prisons in the U.S. territories. And we go deeper to provide further detail on *why* people in the various systems of confinement are locked up.

While the numbers in each slice of this pie chart represent a snapshot of our correctional system, the graphic does not capture the enormous churn in and out of our correctional facilities and therefore the many more lives that are affected by the criminal justice system.

 In addition to the 636,000 people released from prisons each year, <u>over *11 million* people cycle through local jails each year</u>. Jail churn is particularly high because at any given moment a majority of the people in local jails have not been convicted and are in jail because they are either too poor to afford bail and are being held pretrial, or because they have just been arrested and will make bail in the next few hours or days. The remainder of the people in jail — almost 200,000 — is serving time for minor offenses, generally misdemeanors with sentences under a year.

With a sense of the big picture, a natural follow-up question might be: how many people are locked up for a drug offense? While the data doesn't give us a complete answer, we know that almost half a million adults and children are locked up because their most significant offense was a drug offense.

 The data confirms that nonviolent drug convictions are a <u>defining characteristic of the *federal* prison system</u>, but play only a <u>supporting role at the state</u> and local levels. Critically, while drugs are the most significant offense for only a minority of people in state and local facilities, there are 1.6 million drug arrests each year, giving residents of over-policed communities <u>criminal records</u>, which then serve to increase sentences imposed for any future offenses and have many other damaging effects.

All of this offense data comes with an important set of caveats. A person in prison for multiple offenses is reported only for the most serious offense so, for example, there are people in prison for "violent" offenses whose time in prison is extended by the fact that they were also convicted of a drug offense.

Further, almost all convictions are the result of plea bargains, where people plead guilty to a lesser offense — an offense perhaps of a different category or one that they may not have actually committed.

 And many of these categories are nowhere near as clear as the labels imply. For example, "murder" is generally considered being an extremely serious offense, but that broad category groups together the rare group of serial killers, with people who committed acts that are unlikely for reasons of circumstance or <u>advanced age</u> to ever happen again, with offenses that the average American would not consider being murder at all.

For example, the felony murder rule says that if someone dies during the commission of a felony, everyone involved is as guilty of murder as the person who pulled the trigger. Driving a getaway car during a bank robbery where someone was accidentally killed is indeed a serious offense, but few people would really consider that to be murder.

Now, armed with the big picture of how many people are locked up in the United States in the various types of facilities and for what offenses and we need to determine why that factor has the tendency to increase, and we'll have a better foundation to go in order the concept of the Preventive Program of the Criminal Behaviors.

Chapter # 4

"Creation of Racism Offense"

Convert the racism in a phantasmagoric idea that you can put in any event. When somebody besides you, then,   he or she doesn't work to full fill the task requirements work, and you express your disagreement, you 're racist. If you don't show a preference to the black people, you're a racist. If you don't like your daughter married with the black people, you're racist.

The concept of the social prejudice were used to neutralize conservative concepts, with Bogardus' theory of Social Distance appeared in the 1940s by Social Psychologists member of the Frankfort School.

The Social Distance is a measure of social separation between groups caused by perceived or real differences between groups of people as defined by well-known social categories. It manifests across a variety of social categories, including class, race and ethnicity, culture, nationality, religion, gender and sexuality, and age, among others. Sociologists recognize three key types of social distance: affective, normative, and interactive.

They study it through a variety of research methods, including ethnography and participant observation, surveys, interviews, and daily route mapping, among other techniques.

 Studies on social prejudice were used to neutralize conservative concepts. Bogardus' theory of social distance appeared in the 1940s by Social Psychologists members of the Frankfort School.

The enemy was attentive to create problems with the racial minority in the United States, they supported the emerging leadership of a religious leader to defend the civil rights of African Americans prepared conditions to eliminate it and blame to the impersonal concept, the Invisible Government.

Published by Mitrokhin and other Soviet defectors and retired KGB files, as well as the own Commission of murders of the Congress, have been light on three major political killings, John F. Kennedy, Robert F. Kennedy, and Martin Luther King. The coldness of analysis which adds the dimension of time that separates us from the event to analyze came to the conclusion that this tragic incident as well, as other political assassinations in the United States have been planned by our enemy and the objectives very precise to obtain them after the deaths of these three important Americans.

Specifically, the contribution of the assassination of Rev. Martin Luther King assassinations in the United States have been planned by our enemy and objectives very precise to obtain them some advantages after the deaths of these three important Americans.

The Congress through the Commission of murders investigated deaths of John F. Kennedy, Robert F. Kennedy, and Rev. Martin Luther King. In all three cases, there was participation of the Soviet Union showed. The case of the Rev. Luther King was sealed for 50 years. The evidences were scandalous. Let's learn from these cases as the enemy has worked to destroy us, but not assimilate even as they work, and above all, we must keep us United and fight for our country. Before and after of the Civil Right Act signed by President Lyndon Johnson the Communist Party's Agenda had been creating and reviving all kinds of conflicts between blacks and whites. Many events with different tones have been increased in the everyday News on our radio, TV, and newspapers. This argument is the most commonly used by the enemies, but they 'never be fair and will never talk about how to resolve the problems with good will?

Of every 10 marriages in the United States, 4 are interracial since 2015. To continue creating a barrier between races is part of the task of Marxist subversion like said Michelle Obama "to create a mess."

Chapter #5

Point Three "Continue Change to Create Confusion"

"One does not establish a dictatorship in order to safeguard a revolution; one makes a revolution in order to establish a dictatorship" George Orwell

Typical Liberal Presidential Campaign Slogans

Year	Candidate	Slogan
2008	Barack Obama	Change We Can
2008	Barack Obama	Change We Need
2008	Barack Obama	Hope
2008	Barack Obama	Yes, We Can!

POINT # 3

Continue change to create Confusion

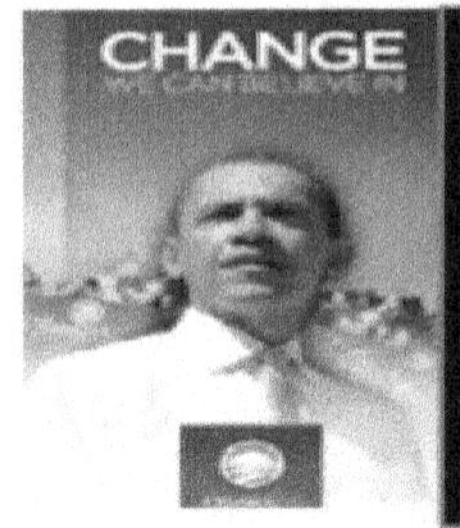

LIES, LIES, and MORE LIES
OFFER GREAT FUTURE EXPECTATIVE AND
PAY WITH MISERY AND DEATH.
PROMOTION THE COMMUNISM AS THE
NEW GLOBAL ORDER

Resulting in frustration and mass misguidance, leading to the Civil War and Crisis

ED PRIDA'S DESIGN

The radical candidate, selected as priority messages in his political campaign; "The Change" because, he knows creating expectation with the change gets support of many more persons, almost without much thinking, any individual can accept the change, the hope to improve, this is part of the Human Being repertory of believing, established by the practice of the Life. The Hope is an universal concept, very wide and very deep, with a different connotation in each personality, but always procures the feeling to improve the status.

The Marxist, have used this Human Being natural drive to involve many in this massive ideology and after manipulating them in their political interests, to create a false expectation about getting the property of your neighbors easily. How do resolve our problem with the Marxist criteria? Perfect example gave by Mike or Michelle Obama.

Why would former First Lady Michelle Obama focus all of her energy on running for President of the United States, when she could instead commit herself to the far more impactful work of creating an army of liberals who think, act and — most importantly — vote just like her?

Speaking at Klick Health's Muse event in New York on Tuesday, Business Insider reported that Obama said that she believes that a presidential race would be a distraction from the crucial <u>task</u> of "creating thousands of messes.

" She never minds to resolve problem, she know how to create messes, deaths, and crisis. The Crisis is the Express Way to the Civil War, for this reason, they want to take your Guns."

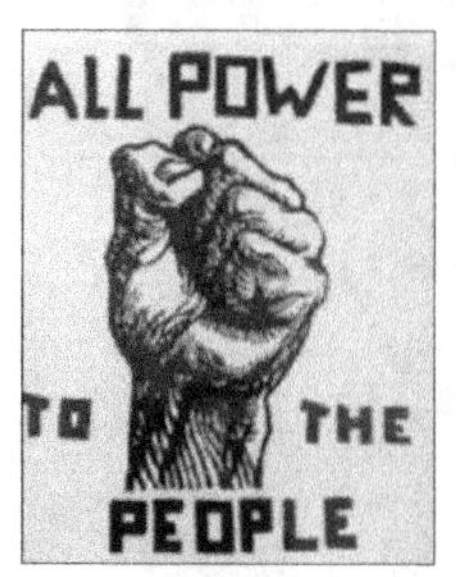

Michelle Obama Red Army…we're watching the result

The Obama Foundation's Agenda and Obama's wife spoke about her point of view, she said. "They're tired of watching us do the same old thing and expect different results. So I'm optimistic about the future.

There are some bright young people out there doing some amazing things." "bright young people out there" are restricted to those young Americans who think, act and vote like she does. She enforced her reasons "This is why I'm not going to run for president. Because I think it's a better investment to invest in creating thousands of messes." She will use her time would be better spent installing like-minded young leaders across the country. "We don't need just one, we need thousands and thousands," she declared. "Thousands and thousands" of duplicate Michelle Obamas would mean that a horde of political thinkers who see the world purely in terms of race relations would descend upon Washington D.C.

   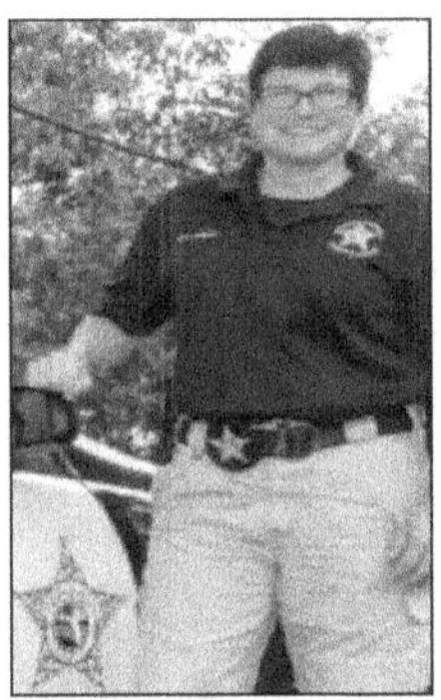

The Michelle Obama's Plan had prepared a team of "emergency cadres" to create "mass agitation", she said "We don't want one young leader,

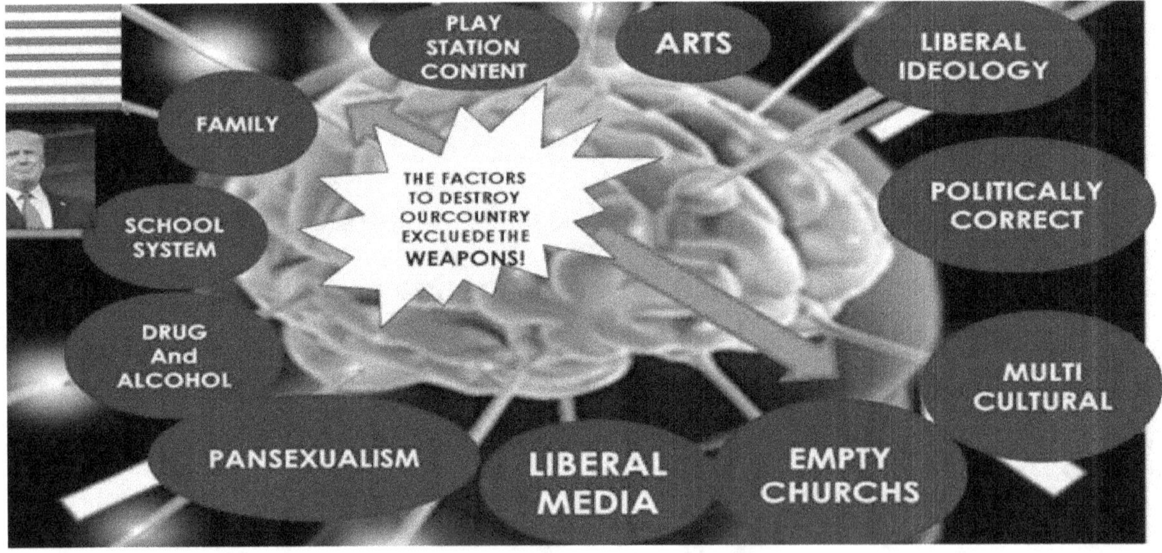

we want hundreds of thousands leaders and create much "messes" around the country every day….

Forget about the hundreds of thousands who perished fighting in the Civil War to abolish slavery, the "greatest generation" who resisted tyranny in Europe and Asia, or the Civil Rights Movement of the 1960s that made it possible for her husband to run for president. Michelle believes that America needs more people who believe that their country was a disgusting cesspool of bigots and xenophobes until the 44th President was inaugurated.

If it were up to the former first lady — and the young people, she wants to see elected to power — Congress would be less "gray and white" because a lack of diversity makes people distrust the political process. She explained her thinking last fall, saying:

At the State of the Union address… when you are in the room what you can see is this real dichotomy. It's a feeling of color almost.

On one side of the room is literally gray and white. Literally, that is the color palette on one side of the room. On the other side of the room, there are

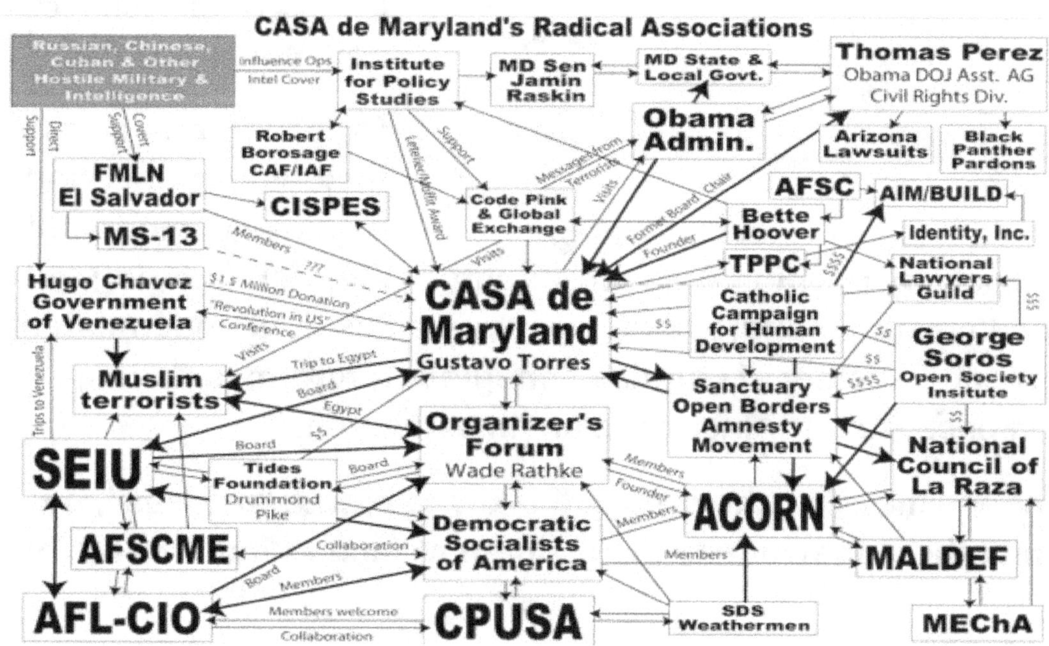

yellows and blues and whites and greens. Physically, there's a difference in color, in the tone, because on one side all men, all white, on the other side some woman, some people of color.

No wonder, then, that Barack Obama — the first "post-racial" president — only succeeded in deepening the racial divide in America. Thanks to his wife, Americans can look forward to "thousands and thousands" of like-minded racial agitators assuming positions of power and destruction in the future. The main political reserve of the radical communist is the Casa of Maryland.

Changing the political face of America

Although the former first lady failed to provide details about how she planned to accomplish her ambitious cloning project, anyone familiar with the liberal agenda can guess what she has in store for America. The Marxists with different names have been committed to this goal for decades following step by step United States Communist Party and Moscow order.

Honor Members

- The organization received $1.5 million dollars from Venezuelan dictator Hugo Chavez. He also received donations from CITGO then owned by the Venezuelan dictatorship and member of CASA.
- Soros, the Hungarian who has sworn to destroy the United States, is also a donor to CASA. Other affiliates of this Maryland House led by Tom Perez are the FMLN, the Salvadoran communist guerrillas,
- The Communist Party of USA (CPUSA), the Maras Salvatruchas (MS-13) who offered $50,000 dollars to anyone who would murder an ICE policeman, Tom Perez was director when that offer occurred)
- ACORN, that Democratic organization that instructed illegals to commit fraud and vote in the elections. Its director, the Democrat, Bertha Lewis proposed socialism for the United States.
- The terrorist organization of the Muslim Brothers also belongs to The Maryland HOUSE. It is also part of that cove Code Pink/Global Exchange, which offered six hundred thousand dollars ($600,000) to the terrorists who fought against the US Marines in Fallujah, Iraq.
- The Committee of Solidarity with the people of Salvador (CISPES) founded and directed by Salvadoran communist leaders; the American Friends Service Committee (AFSC), this communist organization, raised the unilateral disarmament of the United States. All of them were founders of the Maryland HOUSE.

On paper, this plan includes engineering a massive <u>demographic shift</u> in America. By opening America's southern border, ignoring federal authority and creating hundreds of sanctuary cities, and undermining every meaningful attempt at genuine immigration reform is no more immigration because our Americans are in extinction.

The student and massive shooters is the key to create "messes", but the real reason of this behavior has many different factors induced by the leftist.

Michelle Obama once <u>called</u> the resistance against the oppressive act of asking voters to verify their identity "the march of our time" and "the sit-in of our day."

Ref:: <u>https://www.aol.com/article/news/2018/03/02/michelle-obama-wants-to-create-thousands-of-mes-and-shes-not-interested-in-running-for-president/23375516/</u>

Compare the Communist Goals to know the Subversion Advances

1. U.S. acceptance of coexistence as the only alternative to atomic war.
2. U.S. willingness to capitulate in preference to engaging in atomic war.
3<u>. Develop the illusion that total disarmament [by] the United States would be a demonstration of moral strength.</u>
4. Permit free trade between all nations regardless of Communist affiliation and regardless of whether items could be used for war.
5. Extension of long-term loans to Russia and Soviet satellites.
6. <u>Provide American aid to all nations regardless of Communist domination.</u>
7. <u>Grant recognition of Red China. Admission of Red China to the U.N.</u>
8. Set up East and West Germany as separate states in spite of Khrushchev's promise in 1955 to settle the German question by free elections under supervision of the U.N.
9. Prolong the conferences to ban atomic tests because the United States has agreed to suspend tests if negotiations are in progress.
10. Allow all Soviet satellites individual representation in the U.N.
11. Promote the U.N. as the only hope for mankind. If its charter is rewritten, demand that it be set up as a one-world government with its own independent armed forces. (Some Communist leaders believe the world can be taken over as easily by the U.N. as by Moscow. Sometimes these two centers compete as they are now doing in the Congo.)
12. <u>Resist any attempt to outlaw the Communist Party.</u>
13. <u>Do away with all loyalty oaths.</u>
14. <u>Continue giving Russia access to the U.S. Patent Office.</u>
15. <u>Capture one or both political parties in the United States</u>.
16. Use technical decisions of the courts to weaken basic American institutions by claiming their activities violate civil rights.

17. <u>Get control of the schools</u>. Use them as transmission belts for socialism and current Communist propaganda. Soften the curriculum. Get control of teachers' associations. Put the party line in textbooks.
18. Gain control of all student newspapers.
19. <u>Use student riots to foment public protests against programs or organizations which are under Communist attack</u>.
20. <u>Infiltrate the press. Get control of book-review assignments, editorial writing, policymaking positions</u>.
21. <u>Gain control of key positions in radio, TV, and motion pictures</u>.
22. Continue discrediting American culture by degrading all forms of artistic expression. An American Communist cell was told to <u>"eliminate all good sculpture from parks and buildings, substitute shapeless, awkward and meaningless forms."</u>
23. Control art critics and directors of art museums. "Our plan is to promote ugliness, repulsive, meaningless art."
24. Eliminate all laws governing obscenity by calling them "censorship" and a violation of free speech and free press.
25. Break down cultural standards of morality by promoting pornography and obscenity in books, magazines, motion pictures, radio, and TV.
26. <u>Present homosexuality, degeneracy and promiscuity as "normal, natural, healthy."</u>
27. <u>Infiltrate the churches and replace revealed religion with "social" religion. Discredit the Bible and emphasize the need for intellectual maturity which does not need a "religious crutch."</u>
28. <u>Eliminate prayer or any phase of religious expression in the schools on the ground that it violates the principle of "separation of church and state."</u>
29. <u>Discredit the American Constitution by calling it inadequate, old-fashioned, out of step with modern needs, a hindrance to cooperation between nations on a worldwide basis.</u>
30. <u>Discredit the American Founding Fathers. Present them as selfish aristocrats who had no concern for the "common man."</u>
31. <u>Belittle all forms of American culture and discourage the</u> teaching of American history on the ground that it was only a minor part of the "big

picture." Give more emphasis to Russian history since the Communists took over.

32. Support any socialist movement to give centralized control over any part of the culture–education, social agencies, welfare programs, mental health clinics, etc.

33. Eliminate all laws or procedures which interfere with the operation of the Communist apparatus.

34. Eliminate the House Committee on Un-American Activities.

35. Discredit and eventually dismantle the FBI.

36. Infiltrate and gain control of more unions.

37. Infiltrate and gain control of big business.

38. Transfer some of the powers of arrest from the police to social agencies. Treat all behavioral problems as psychiatric disorders which no one but psychiatrists can understand [or treat].

39. Dominate the psychiatric profession and use mental health laws as a means of gaining coercive control over those who oppose Communist goals.

40. Discredit the family as an institution. Encourage promiscuity and easy divorce.

41. Emphasize the need to raise children away from the negative influence of parents. Attribute prejudices, mental blocks and retarding of children to suppressive influence of parents.

42. Create the impression that violence and insurrection are legitimate aspects of the American tradition; that students and special-interest groups should rise up and use ["] united force["] to solve economic, political or social problems.

43. Overthrow all colonial governments before native populations are ready for self-government.

44. Internationalize the Panama Canal.

45. Repeal the Connally reservation so the United States cannot prevent the World Court

Read more at http://www.beliefnet.com/columnists/watchwomanonthewall/2011/04/the-45-communist-goals-as-read-into-the-congressional-record-1963.html#yEMDmqx6QHSYuTyy.99

This the way how to change America by the Liberal, they don't have Plans to resolve our problems like a country, they want to create more problems…Karl Marx, Vladimir I. Lenin, Fidel Castro, and Ernesto Guevara did the same…create problems.

DEMOCRATY PARTY
now public branch of Communisty Party
and Jihaad

- Perez Dropped Voter Intimidation Charges Against Black Panthers Who Brought Weapons to a Polling Place
- Perez Doesn't Think White People Are Protected Under the Voting Rights Act
- Perez Abandoned a Whistleblower Lawsuit That Cost Taxpayers Millions
- He Used a Private Email Address to Dodge Accountability
- He Continues to Ignore and Mislead Congress

GEORGE SOROS'S PRODUCTION

Soros, George & Open Society Institute

- Funder of the Left
- Financially supports over 150 leftist organizations and causes[59]
- Creator of the Shadow Party[60]
- Supports all open borders & amnesty initiatives
- Provided funding to CASA
- Prominent member of Coalition for Comprehensive Immigration Reform[61]

Soros investment strategies have caused currency devaluations and economic collapse in countries all over the world. His hedge fund operations are shrouded in secrecy, but he has been convicted of insider trading in France, and is persona-non-grata in Indonesia and other countries whose economies have been ruined by his currency manipulation schemes.

Soros' investment track record was likely earned with insider information. The fact that his operation has not been shut down by RICO statutes, as Michael Milliken's junk bond operations were, speaks volumes about his malevolent grip on Washington, DC, particularly within the Democrat Party.

Chapter 6

The Teaching the Sex and Homosexuality to Children

Note.- This chapter and others are not directed against people who suffer from dysphoria with their sex or use their imagination to stop being what their DNA has clearly edited, we consider them sick in need of treatment, and we call attention to stop to those who drive this destructive campaign. This information is aimed at the population knowing this factor as an integral part of the Subversive Plan created and promoted by the enemies of the United States for more than 70 years ago by a group of communist psychologists at the request of the USSR.

Condition gender changes against the will of the parents and much more School Boards are doing in all the Counties and many other instances of our country with the approval of the Three Powers and with much enthusiasm from the Fourth Power Branch, the Press.

The teaching of sex and homosexuality to children

The Psychopathic Disorder converted to social status and his proliferation is a demoralization factor to multiplay the aberration from early ages

Resulting in broken heritage family, control lost by the parents, slashing society, new civil laws, low demographic rate, drug abuse candidate, and a conflicting social role.

There is in the Subversive Plan the method of eliminating the classical forms of education from the very beginning of life in the family setting to hinder sexual identification.   The economic interest has introduced hormonal methods and surgery to try to eliminate the dysphoria against the original sex before the age of 18, without foreseeing that 41% of them later take the suicide route.

The life of all those who suffer from dysphoria due to their sex have a common factor: the real or affective absence of the psychological model of the gender role to imitate and internalize. Others the absence of affection or sexual abuse received from a member of the family or their social group has been the cause of the rejection of their sex. If the origin and sexual dysphoria is psychological; Why then introduce biological methods to mitigate it? It would be useful to compare it with someone with panic to the crocodiles, then remove both eyes so you do not see the crocodiles. But not seeing the crocodiles does not erase their traumatic memory. The psychological conflicts in an individual who makes the decision to cut his penis or breasts, will not disappear with the operation, much less than a woman will get a mustache and beard will be a man.

At the social level, there are more and more complexities with this artificial phenomenon created and promoted and fully coincides with the original objectives, both the Plan of the Frankfurt School and the Communist Party, to destroy the United States.

The recognition of homosexual marriage is an atrocity legal, aberrant because they create more problems than solutions, Laws cannot be complacent; these must be logical and rational. Respect the rights of all those involved. Where the right of others begins, ends ours, considering the interests of the nation as a whole.

If the will of an individual is based on a sexual fantasy by self-denomination with the opposite gender and also provides a social and legal status, we open the door to the possibility of creating a fictitious and abnormal family, which cannot be, in the first instance because a family is formed by parents and children in all species and these lovers of fantasies do not present the biological and psychological requirements to have natural children, therefore, until now the Judges do not have the virtue of the Magic of make a father and a mother two men or two women. The importance of forming a family, without taking into account the nature and the jurisprudence is a serious error, which must be quickly corrected.

The psychological and psychiatric disorder that these individuals carry with pride, simply does not allow them to have a healthy relationship with an "adopted child", this child is not a pet, it is not a toy, it is a human being who is being usurped by his right to be a normal human being, which in fact is a carrier of trauma due to the absence of their legitimate and biological parents, needs the protection of society and we must not renounce to protect them despite the political conspiracy that obstructs it.

When the right of adoption is granted to a couple, already de facto dysfunctional by their whim and imagination of pleasure, we are committing a crime against an unprotected creature to even punish it by introducing it into the life of a dysfunctional couple, we are facing a new escalation of aberration with legal guarantee. We enter another cycle of problems and an indolent attitude against the adopted creature which we do not relinquish the duty to defend.

There has never been a public debate to inform the population, because it has not been an interest of the media, to spread the arguments in favor or against to raise awareness of the transcendental importance of the topic.

First of all, we should all know that it is part of an enemy's plan to weaken us in many ways. The consequences of the proliferation of sexual dysphoria in childhood, gender change, marriage of homosexuals, adoption and other lines that civil law gives a fictitious partner, those who control the mainstream media ensure that it does not arrive to the population mass.

The decrease in population is facilitated by abortions and the growth trend of homosexual couples. However, other negative aspects such as the high rate of suicides, drug use, crimes, and penal population are direct consequences associated with this factor.

In addition, the high costs in surgical treatments and medications without positive results. For reasons unknown and alien to science, the Association of American Psychologists, instead of seeking a solution to the multiple psychosocial factors created to make the wave of disasters giant, they support activism in favor of homosexuals. Psychiatrists, clinical and social psychologists must be the shock troop to solve this great problem we face.

All the points of the Subversive Plan of the Frankfurt School and the 45 goals of the Communist Party of the United States, also directed by Moscow, have been successfully fulfilled. Thanks to our Congressmen, Senators, and Judges charged "voluntarily" to materialize the enemy's goals, they still seem blind and deaf to the reality we face.

Scientifically, sexual dysphoria, formerly known as deficient sexual identification, its origin was always known was the result of the absence of an affective and emotional channel between parents and children, whether father or mother must transmit and fertilize with attention and love the implantation of the male or female role of the son/daughter before the age of three. The biological genus is an immutable physical characteristic.   Never a male can be gestated; a female will never produce sperm.

The natural development of sexual identity with its biological sex is a natural and purely psychological process, which comes through learning by imitation, this being the simplest and in turn the most important learning mechanism, of all the species of the animal kingdom and reaches 80% of our knowledge ".

These psychological mechanisms were known by those who planned to increase sexual dysphoria because they do just the opposite, they try to pass the link father-child to school, to the Internet, to TV, etc. eliminating parental and maternal figures from this channel of communication. This bizarre phenomenon has been one of many planned and created by our enemies   ...   to destroy us.   He has demonstrated that this has not been a phenomenon spontaneous from psychosocial development, to the defects of bourgeois or capitalist society like the Marxists and liberals want make us believe that false argument.

As proof that this phenomenon   was introduced with   certainty is in a Psychological War Manual   of the KGB, here are the instructions to give strength to the social image of the   homosexuals

Some schools on the west coast are using a new rule with the clothes: One day the students come with men's clothes, the alternative day,   the male students arrived with the clothes of the females and a hairstyle of feminine cut.

What is the purpose of this rule?

To destroy, create confusion with the ID, sexual identification.   The students are learning that gender differentiation   It is not important, you can "locate and act" with any sex, you only need imagination.

For what, the homosexuals they need be highlighted?   What damages can they do?

The phenomenon of the "massive proliferation of homosexuality" of the population has many advantages for the enemies of the United States.   Morally, one of these aims or objectives is to reach an undifferentiated level on sex, because, in the first age of life, sex has different needs to be exposed, because boys and girls can be confused by their roles and rules.

Before the arrival of the Frankfortt Group in the United States, the classrooms of the schools were separated, between boys and girls.

Special subjects were for males while others were for females congruent with the content and the role of females and males in their next stage, which reinforced from the first stages to reinforce the gender identity of each one through exercise and role in each group, as well as other characteristics of communication between the sexes.

The level of respect, nice, chivalry and differential treatment that should establish patterns of behavior within the establishment of relations between females and males.

These factors were part of the basis of ethical values that the male has developed for the female, the opposite, the female for the male. Examples of the form of social encounter of the couples when they dance, historically the man and the woman each had a very specific role, currently the woman is introduced dancing with another in frank movements of sexual excitement.

When there is no difference of roles, equality is generalized, which is absolutely false, because the nature, biology and psychological expression of each sex are completely different and can be differentiated at any level to compare, but this is not only for the human species, all species have biological differences, behaviors, needs, muscle strength, fur, size, etc. Absolutely differentiated.

Other of the products subversive is to create divergences and conflicts in the family, marriage, the relationship between parents and children, etc.

However, at a social level, progressively   HE   has delineated perfectly since this phenomenon of the gay couples needs to achieve legal recognition, the first marriage, and then adjust all the civil rights that this legal union represents with benefits and inheritance.

On the other hand, these couples, in an unrealistic and impractical, supported just by an imagination. After, they extend the sexual fantasy to an impossible procreation, then they seek in the adoption of innocents the realization of another fantasy, but now playing with a defenseless human being, that they submit to a psychological environment of dysphoria of aberrant fantasies and genres. These children become objects or sex slaves of the supposed guardians or protectors.

There have been many, as we have seen,   tactics used by the enemy to make sexual aberration an epidemic, one of these tactics, in addition to those mentioned above, namely the reinforcement of the role of victim: Method of creation of homosexuality at the social level used by the KGB, taken of a Manual of Psychological Warfare of the KGB.

"We believe that the first thing is to get used to them and make them part of everyday life. <u>Each day becomes more normal and acceptable in the proportion that the stimulus becomes more repeated</u>". <u>Josef Stalin</u>

The victims always have the consideration and the respect; so *they look for the force to occupy the role of victims* illegitimate *and get the consideration and the respect!!!*

The way to numb the spontaneous sensitivity to homosexuality is that many people speak *Much on the subject in terms of acceptance or at least neutral.*

That attitude on the subject gives the impression that public opinion, at least, is neutral, which in terms of psychological warfare, is already won for the other side.   Little has been discussed publicly *between defenders and detractors that could have served to raise adverse and consistent opinions about the consequences of promoting homosexuality.*

The most used method is that in the media, be show or movies a homosexual *appears in a scene,* he *is a "respectable homosexual" and leaves an assimilable image.   But the main thing is to create the monotony of the images until the stimulus does not a negative* attitude or rejection, *like many they say, "until make it boring. "*

This social layer artificially created it mixes with others; Marxists call it antagonistic social factors, which force them politically to reinforce these conflicting individual interests to create the so-called "class struggle"   "

These factors are mixed with great force to create groups in antagonistic sectors, for a conflict of interests, the students against the teachers, the workers against the owners, parents against children, wives against husbands, the long, the days.   We are approaching a crisis that will cause sudden changes in the power groups and their structuring.

Like a man more and more isolated, because those who suffer this impact directly are the family and the groups of belonging, which are becoming increasingly difficult to access and maintain their cohesion to survive thanks to their functionality.

The consequence of this phenomenon is the loss of the emotional and affective value of the human and spiritual relationships inherent and developed by man as a mechanism of integration to social and cultural development.

 Spreading homosexuality is the priority task on the agenda of the left. Hollywood and Disney, infant entertainment industries are intent on driving the epidemic outbreak of homosexuality.

SNOW IS BLACK

Bertrand Russell: Lord Bertrand Russell together the Frankfort School added some new ideas in 1951. The Mass Social Engineering with "The Impact of Science on the Society" and "Physiology and Psychology", he made a description how the propaganda work in the human being. Also, he focused a new concept of Education using Social Psychology's methods of producing an unshakable conviction "SNOW IS BLACK."

He based the education to create a totalitarian new society…everybody in the same line. According to Russell, the influence of the family is obstructive. The new political indoctrination must start before the 10 years old.

The repeated music intoned is very effective to create the best channel of for the indoctrination ideas. At last, he enforced that the opinion "the snow is black" must be held to show a morbid taste of eccentricity. Really the indoctrination of totalitarian regime produce the must absurd ways to understand his social role and his individual performance inside the society. They are unable to adaptation in the free world.

RELIGIOUS PARENTS LOSE CUSTODY OF A TRANSGENDER ADOLESCENT FOR REFUSING HORMONAL TREATMENT.

Religious parents lose custody of transgender teenage daughter for refusing hormonal treatment, by Bradford Richardson - The Washington Times - Tuesday, February 20, 2018, Hamilton County, Ohio, judge took custody of a transgender teenager on Friday because They refused to allow their 17-year-old daughter to undergo hormonal treatments as part of a woman-to-man transition. Judge Sylvia Sieve Hendon granted custody of the teenager to her grandparents, who can make medical decisions for the minor and legally change her name *The Washington Times*

The Sex: Bio-Psychological-Social Factor

Gordon W. Allport,   One of the most brilliant contemporary psychologists, in his book 'Configuration and personality development' explains … 'The sexual instinct in all biological species is a primary impetus to ensure the preservation of the species, with the exclusion of humans and dolphins, sexual activity is not only a reproduction mechanism, but it is a great complexity of external and internal variables of the individual ".

Among the external variables are all the factors outside the body and the mind, but it determines, facilitates or inhibits the sexual instinct and the consent of the couple (physical environment, religion, social status, etc.) internal factors contain sexual impulses, this involves a portion of purely biological forces such as hormones, neurotransmitters, psychodynamic states, psyche, toxic,., but act in conjunction with other mechanisms and purely psychological, that carry the historical and social character of each person (positive or negative) and project on the selection of the partner and the peculiarities of the sexual act itself.

If we summarize the idea, we can conclude that sex is nothing more than the projection of an intimate event of the personalities involved, where mutual complacency is centered on defense mechanisms, where bio-gene and psychological needs are reflected among them. The Unresolved conflicts, integrating all these attitudes are determining the quality of affective relationships, this mechanism is common for all types of couples.

The different contributions of the abstraction of thought as delusions or fantasies makes a way for the deviations of behaviors within sexual relations, historically known by the classics of psychology such as sadism, masochism, exhibitionism, fetishism, sexual violence, bestiality, necrophilia, infanticide, these forms of deviations practiced by humans within sexual behavior, in contrast to other species of Creation, since human sexuality is expansive because of the richness of our psyche can be taken to all the levels that thought can reach.

In summary, sexuality can acquire an incredible number of models or shapes,   and each one indicates the mechanism of defense that generates these behaviors, in general, they are no more than defensive mechanisms designed to overcome the conflicts acquired in different stages of personality development in both sexes, each one with its psychological peculiarities. Among them:

- Public-Hidden
- Active-passive
- Compulsive obsessions with respect to some thought
- Sublimated (Jealous and Addict)

- **Fuzzy (Confusion of the Self)**
- **Specify (With a Person)**
- **Altruistic (Identification with   other   person)**
- **Friendly (Circumstantial Complacency)**
- **Sadism (To produce pain or frustration)**
- **Protection (Security)**
- **Adulation (Subordination)**
- **Superficial (Limited)**
- **Repressed (Unconscious produces addictions)**
- **Peripheral   (Limited)**
- **Central (Single Satisfaction)**
- **Transitory (Eventual Episodes)**
- **Persistent (Thinking of Permanent Self-Punishment)**
- **Esthetics (Attraction for Beauty)**
- **Intellectual (Rationalization)**

Many forms or models as individuals can exist, it can also be said that each of these models can be perfectly adjusted to heterosexual relationships, because each one designs and provides its historical-psycho-social characteristics in the sexual act itself and also It will determine if the act is isolated or stays for one episode or more, whether it succeeds or not, if it meets expectations.

Can accept that the choice of the couple is determined by the historical configuration of each personality, which leads us to think that, if certain variables are introduced into the psychological and social environment, can influence what type of partner the individual selects or accepts to project their "sexual instincts", therefore, if we change the way in which the environment favors a certain type of couple, we can eradicate this psychopathological category at a social level.

Result of children adopted by Couples: Suicide

The study, prepared by the professor Mark Rangenerius, a sociologist at the Research Center of University   of Texas, along with eight social scientists from different North American universities, concludes that young people who have grown up in homes formed by same-sex couples are more likely to suffer from mental problems, less stable relationships and higher rates of criminality.

> ## Suicide rates
>
> •LGBTQ youth contemplate suicide at a 2.6 times greater rate than straight-identified youth.
> •LGBTQ youth actively plan suicide at a 2.6 times greater rate than straight-identified youth.
> •LGBTQ youth attempt suicide at a 4.0 times greater rate than straight-identified youth.
> •LGBTQ youth require medical attention for suicide attempts at a 5.1 times greater rate than straight-identified youth.

"The statistics show with some clarity that children raised by gay parents or   Lesbians are, on average, at a significant disadvantage when compared to children raised by their biological parents, married, in intact families, "says Regnerus in his report.

The 'Study of the *New Family Structures Study* ', whose contents were validated and disseminated by the prestigious scientific Journal   *Social Science Research*, has been based on the analysis of thousands of data obtained with a survey conducted the year 2011 to 2,988 young people between 18 to 39 years.

In the sample, there were people raised by adults, biological parents or not, who at some point in their lives had or maintained a homosexual relationship at the time of the survey.

The survey was also applied to young people of similar profiles, but raised in other family environments such as natural, adoptive, divorced or single-parent families. The number of interviewees, diversity and statistical rigor make this survey the most reliable measurement instrument today.

The risks of growing up in a gay or lesbian family

The conclusions of the study conducted by Regnerus, where it is stated that children who are adopted or raised by same-sex couples are exposed to serious risks, leave no room for much doubt. "Children raised in homosexual homes have a lower average income level when they are adults, and suffer from more physical health problems and mental, as well as greater instability in their relationships, "he warns.

 Source:
https://www.google.com/search?hl=en&authuser=0&tbm=isch&source=hp&biw=940&bih=318&ei=Aru2WtDbC YTYzgLc_77QBA&q=lesbian+and+gay+suicidadl+statistic+&oq=lesbian+and+gay+suicidadl+statistic+&gs_l=im g.12...3484.15904.0.18788.38.6.0.32.32.0.95.304.4.4.0....0...1ac.1.64.img..2.8.317.0..0j35i39k1.0.zn2VZK35Q6k#imgr c=vo9x8BOSfZqgdM

Also, 40% of children of gay or lesbian couples have contracted a sexually transmitted disease, while in heterosexual couples the percentage is 8%. 12% of respondents who grew up with same-sex couples have thought about suicide, compared to 5% of children raised by a man and a woman.

The children of same-sex couples, the study continues, resort more easily to psychotherapy and require greater social assistance (19% versus 8%). They are often unemployed (28% against 8%), are usually poorer, less healthy, more prone to smoking and crime.

Professor Regnerus pointed out that children of lesbian couples differ in a statistically significant level from children raised in intact biological families in 25 of the 40 aspects measured by the Study. Similarly, the children of gay couples show a statistically significant degree in 11 of the 40 aspects measured compared to the rest of the families.

The findings of the academic group led by Prof. Regnerus categorically question the validity of the 59 studies cited by the Psychological Association American (APA) that, with a much smaller number of cases and less data crossing, affirmed that there were no disadvantages for children raised by gay or lesbian parents.

On the contrary, the report takes stock of the studies recorded during the last 10 years and corresponding academic discussion on the subject, noting that none of these studies is methodologically strong in order to sustain the position of the APA.

Who defends the rights of these violated children?

Given the evidence of the conclusions of the Prof. Regnerus study, the question of who defends the violated rights of children growing up in   homes with same-sex couples

Ref. Http://www.forumlibertas.com/Nuevo-informed-los-hijos-de-parejas-gays-o-lesbianas-estan-en-desventaja-ante-los-criados-por-padres-biologicos/

Promiscuity of those of homosexual couples

A scientific study entitled: "A Comparative Demographic and Sexual Profile of Older Homosexually Active Men",   published in the _Journal of Sex Research_ and conducted on 2583 homosexuals, that the minimum values of the population 10.2-15.7% of them had had in their lives between 501 and 1000 sexual partners; a maximum 10.2-15.7% had had more than 1000 sexual partners .

The data shows that even in 1997 it was relatively difficult to get a couple and highlights the number of couples they were able to get. Homosexual activity shows that it does not offer stability and even much worse to adopt children in such type of home. This population group only needs sexuality without responsibility in an open and liquid way, this shows that much less can constitute an acceptable environment for adoption.

 LGBT activists push us...!

  Dr. Paul McHugh, professor of psychiatry at the Johns Hopkins University School of Medicine for 26 years and a pioneer in sex surgery to treat gender dysphoria. When he analyzed the results, he concluded that the procedures performed did not bring any benefits to his patients and stoped the surgery since 1970. Today, he recommends that the dysphoria gender have a psychosocial adjustment treatment like the other mental illnesses.

Dr. Paul McHugh   and Lawrence S. Mayer, biostatistician and   Epidemiologist, published in "The New Atlantis" a report entitled "Sexuality and Gender: findings   from   the biological, psychological, and

Social Sciences factors, "where it is demonstrated that the claims and affirmations of the LGBT movement" are not based on scientific evidence. "

"The dysphoria gender, a sense of incongruence between the biological sex and one's own, accompanied by clinically significant distress or deterioration, sometimes treated in adults by hormones or surgery, but there is little scientific evidence that these therapeutic interventions have psychological benefits. "

Diabolic Sex Plan supported by the Medical Institution

Despite its modest political gains, favored by the Democratic Party, the transgender movement has rapidly institutionalized its ideology in leading medical institutions and research universities,   For example, Boston Children's Hospital is recommended as "the first major program in the United States focused on transgender children and adolescents" in 2007.

<u>**"Today, more than 45 pediatric gender clinics have opened their doors to the children of our nation in the last ten years."   It is worth asking, Ethics or Money?**</u>

People with dysphoria <u>gender 41% take the suicide behavior</u> as the definitive solution for the problem what a minority portion of our society is

pushing with the support of the communist forces.

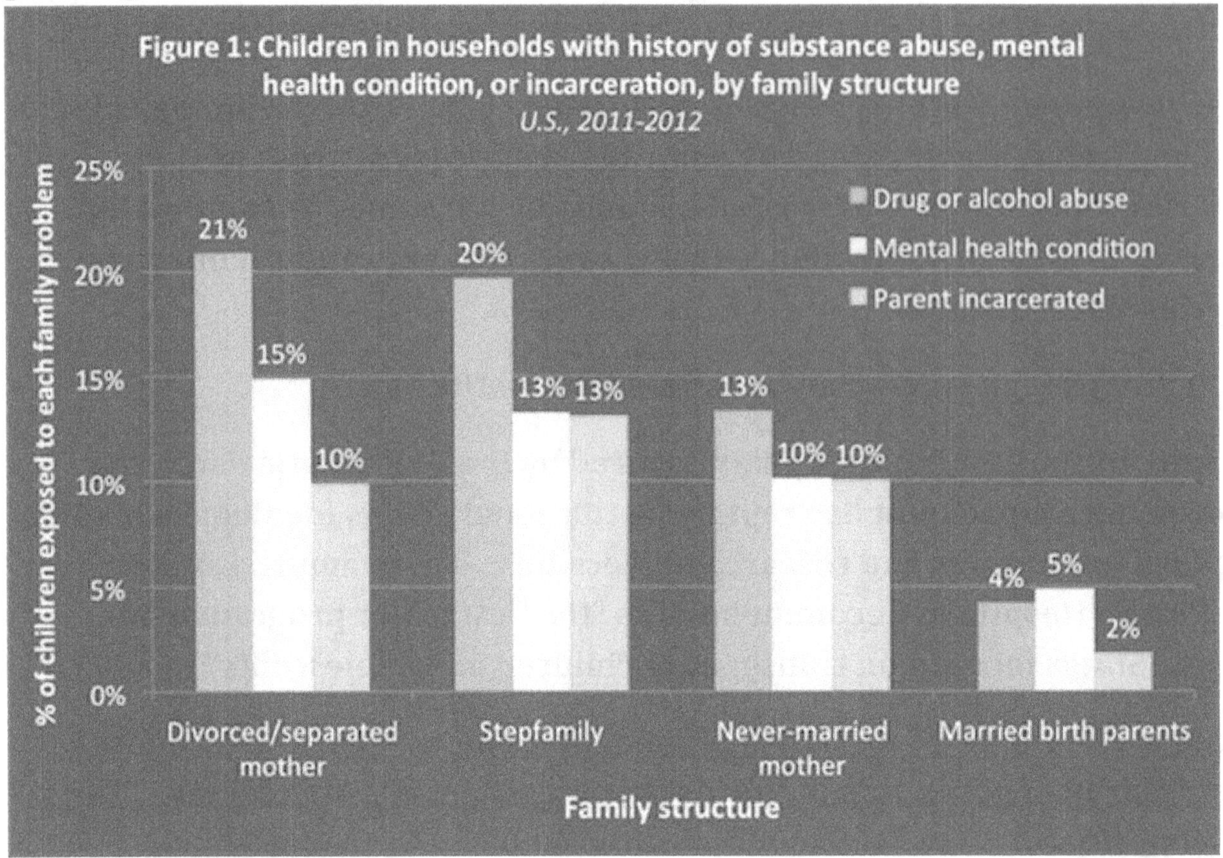

It is very important to take control of where the activists are hurting Humanity by imposing their absurd ideology especially on the children of now who will be the adults of tomorrow. How long would human life exist on the planet with the new generations?

The proposed strategy to "one sex society" requires a four-part process and is based on medical treatments; (as part of the business) after the "gender dysphoria" that they themselves induce is diagnosed, as we have already seen as an important part of the Subversive Plan.

First, children should be encouraged to make a social transition if they express a "consistent, insistent and persistent" identification with the opposite sex to which nature endows them. Among other things, the social transition consists of a new name, it is called Robert, we will call it "Rose Margaret", a new gender pronoun was He will be She, a new wardrobe,

wore trousers after a miniskirt, access to the bathrooms and changing rooms of the opposite sex, to put on makeup and sit down to urinate.

Secondly, as children approach puberty, they are treated with hormonal medications so that the reproductive organs in the body they imagine they do not develop.

Third, as children reach adolescence, they should receive the "sex hormones of the opposite sex: estrogen for the child and testosterone for the girl, to simulate the pubertal development in the body" imagined by the victim ".

The final stage of the transition occurs around age 18 when they become eligible for surgical procedures that replace external genitalia and secondary sexual characteristics with those that imitate the sex that their fantasy has chosen.

Parents caught by the subversive activism of the "gender" are led to think that if they do not follow the induced fantasies, their children will make the decision to commit suicide.

The future of this child could be saved from the jaws of suicide, if from the first manifestations of tastes, inappropriate gestures and attitudes incongruent with their biological sex, a psychotherapeutic treatment is applied to the family, sport and school group and, the 95% of these children " dysphoric " can <u>re-identify with their biological sex and get a normal development.</u>

 Rectifying the course and stopping the Subversive Plan must be an urgent task to preserve the Planet from the extinction of the species, the most important species of the Planet.

The American College of Pediatrician stated an official communication against the ideology of gender.
1. Human sexuality is an objective biological binary trait: "XY" and "XX" are genetic markers of male and female, respectively – not genetic markers of a disorder. The norm for human design is to be conceived either male or female. Human sexuality is binary by design with the obvious purpose being the reproduction and flourishing of

our species. This principle is self-evident. The exceedingly rare disorders of sex development (DSDs), including but not limited to testicular feminization and congenital adrenal hyperplasia, are all medically identifiable deviations from the sexual binary norm and are rightly recognized as disorders of human design. Individuals with DSDs (also referred to as "intersex") do not constitute a third sex.[1]

2. No one is born with a gender. Everyone is born with a biological sex. Gender (an awareness and sense of oneself as male or female) is a sociological and psychological concept; not an objective biological one. No one is born with an awareness of themselves as male or female; this awareness develops over time and, like all developmental processes, may be derailed by a child's subjective perceptions, relationships, and adverse experiences from infancy forward. People who identify as "feeling like the opposite sex" or "somewhere in between" do not comprise a third sex. They remain biological men or biological women.[2,3,4]

3. A person's belief that he or she is something they are not is, at best, a sign of confused thinking. When an otherwise healthy biological boy believes he is a girl, or an otherwise healthy biological girl believes she is a boy, an objective psychological problem exists that lies in the mind, not the body, and it should be treated as such. These children suffer from gender dysphoria. Gender dysphoria (GD), formerly listed as Gender Identity Disorder (GID), is a recognized mental disorder in the most recent edition of the Diagnostic and Statistical Manual of the American Psychiatric Association (DSM-5).[5] The psychodynamic and social learning theories of GD/GID have never been disproved.[2,4,5]

4. Puberty is not a disease and puberty-blocking hormones can be dangerous. Reversible or not, puberty-blocking hormones induce a state of disease – the absence of puberty – and inhibit growth and fertility in a previously biologically healthy child.[6]

5. According to the DSM-5, as many as 98% of gender-confused boys and 88% of gender-confused girls eventually accept their biological sex after naturally passing through puberty.[5]

6. Pre-pubertal children diagnosed with gender dysphoria may be given puberty blockers as young as eleven and will require cross-sex hormones in later adolescence to continue impersonating the opposite sex. These children will never be able to conceive any genetically related children even via artificial reproductive technology. In addition, cross-sex hormones (testosterone and estrogen) are associated with dangerous health risks including but not limited to cardiac disease, high blood pressure, blood clots, stroke, diabetes, and cancer.[7,8,9,10,11]

7. Rates of suicide are nearly twenty times greater among adults who use cross-sex hormones and undergo sex reassignment surgery, even in Sweden which is among the most LGBTQ – affirming countries.[12] What compassionate and reasonable person would condemn young children to this fate knowing that after puberty as

many as 88% of girls and 98% of boys will eventually accept reality and achieve a state of mental and physical health?

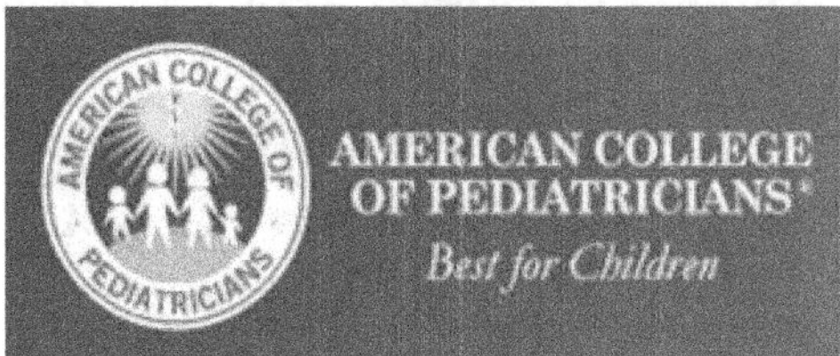

The American College of Pediatricians urges healthcare professionals, educators and legislators to reject all policies that condition children to accept as normal a life of chemical and surgical impersonation of the opposite sex. Facts – not ideology – determine reality.

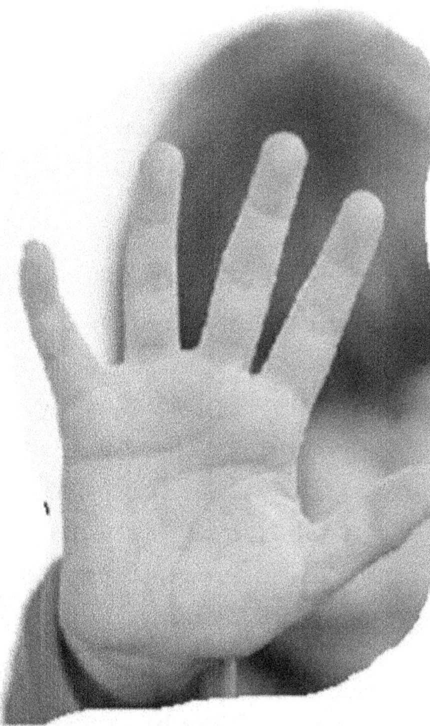

8. Conditioning children into believing a lifetime of chemical and surgical impersonation of the opposite sex is normal and healthful is child abuse. Endorsing gender discordance as normal via public education and legal policies will confuse children and parents, leading more children to present to "gender clinics" where they will be given puberty-blocking drugs. This, in turn, virtually ensures they will "choose" a lifetime of carcinogenic and otherwise toxic cross-sex hormones, and likely consider unnecessary surgical mutilation of their healthy body parts as young adults.

The media never explain, never lets know opinions anti-homosexuality. For example, the American College of Pediatrician stated an official communication against the ideology of gender.

1. Human sexuality is an objective biological binary trait: "XY" and "XX" are genetic markers of male and female, respectively – not genetic markers of a disorder. The norm for human design is to be conceived either male or female.

 Human sexuality is binary by design with the obvious purpose being the reproduction and flourishing of our species. This principle is self-evident. The exceedingly rare disorders of sex development (DSDs), including but not limited to testicular feminization and congenital adrenal hyperplasia, are all medically identifiable deviations from the sexual binary norm and are rightly recognized as disorders of human design. Individuals with DSDs (also referred to as "intersex") do not constitute a third sex.1

2. No one is born with a gender. Everyone is born with a biological sex. Gender (an

awareness and sense of oneself as male or female) is a sociological and psychological concept; not an objective biological one. No one is born with an awareness of themselves as male or female; this awareness develops over time and, like all developmental processes, may be derailed by a child's subjective perceptions, relationships, and adverse experiences from infancy forward. People who identify as "feeling like the opposite sex" or "somewhere in between" do not comprise a third sex. They remain biological men or biological women.[2,3,4]

3. A person's belief that he or she is something they are not is, at best, a sign of confused thinking. When an otherwise healthy biological boy believes he is a girl, or an otherwise healthy biological girl believes she is a boy, an objective psychological problem exists that lies in the mind, not the body, and it should be treated as such. These children suffer from gender dysphoria. Gender dysphoria (GD), formerly listed as Gender Identity Disorder (GID), is a recognized mental disorder in the most recent edition of the Diagnostic and Statistical Manual of the American Psychiatric Association (DSM-5).[5] The psychodynamic and social learning theories of GD/GID have never been disproved.[2,4,5]

4. Puberty is not a disease and puberty-blocking hormones can be dangerous. Reversible or not, puberty-blocking hormones induce a state of disease – the absence of puberty – and inhibit growth and fertility in a previously biologically healthy child.[6]

5. According to the DSM-5, as many as 98% of gender-confused boys and 88% of gender-confused girls eventually accept their biological sex after naturally passing through puberty.[5]

6. Pre-pubertal children diagnosed with gender dysphoria may be given puberty blockers as young as eleven and will require cross-sex hormones in later adolescence to continue impersonating the opposite sex. These children will never be able to conceive any genetically related children even via artificial reproductive technology. In addition, cross-sex hormones (testosterone and estrogen) are associated with dangerous health risks including but not limited to cardiac disease, high blood pressure, blood clots, stroke, diabetes, and cancer.[7,8,9,10,11]

7. Rates of suicide are nearly twenty times greater among adults who use cross-sex hormones and undergo sex reassignment surgery, even in Sweden which is among

the most LGBTQ – affirming countries.12 What compassionate and reasonable person would condemn young children to this fate knowing that after puberty as many as 88% of girls and 98% of boys will eventually accept reality and achieve a state of mental and physical health?

8. Conditioning children into believing a lifetime of chemical and surgical impersonation of the opposite sex is normal and healthful is child abuse. Endorsing gender discordance as normal via public education and legal policies will confuse children and parents, leading more children to present to "gender clinics" where they will be given puberty-blocking drugs. This, in turn, virtually ensures they will "choose" a lifetime of carcinogenic and otherwise toxic cross-sex hormones, and likely consider unnecessary surgical mutilation of their healthy body parts as young adults.

Michelle A. Cretella, M.D.
President of the American College of Pediatricians (Courtesy)

The result of children adopted by Couples: Suicide
The study, prepared by the prominent professor Mark Rangenerius, a sociologist at the Research Center of University of Texas, along with eight social scientists from different North American universities, concludes that young people who have grown up in homes formed by same-sex couples are more likely to suffer from mental problems, less stable relationships and higher rates of criminality.
"The statistics show with some clarity that children raised by gay parents or Lesbians are, on average, at a significant disadvantage when compared to children raised by their biological parents, married, in intact families, "says Regnerus in his report.
The 'Study of the New Family Structures Study ', whose contents were validated and disseminated by the prestigious scientific Journal Social Science Research, has been based on the analysis of thousands of data obtained with a survey conducted the year 2011 to 2,988 young people between 18 to 39 years.
In the sample, there were people raised by adults, biological parents or not, who at some point in their lives had or maintained a homosexual relationship at the time of the survey.
The survey was also applied to young people of similar profiles but raised in other family environments such as natural, adoptive, divorced or single-parent families.
The number of interviewees, diversity and statistical rigor make this survey the most reliable measurement instrument today.
The risks of growing up in a gay or lesbian family
The conclusions of the study conducted by Regnerus, where it is stated that children

who are adopted or raised by same-sex couples are exposed to serious risks, leave no room for much doubt. "Children raised in homosexual homes have a lower average income level when they are adults, and suffer from more physical health problems and mental, as well as greater instability in their relationships, "he warns

Troja's Donkey: Recruitment Gay Campaign

These conceptual "viruses" are "presuppositions or premises" of the sexual dysphoria movement to expand the lesbian and gay epidemic. Each of these false premises try to justify homosexual behaviors as something natural and in fact a part of social development. Each one of these premises is a step for you to accept, first passively and out of curiosity you approach sexual behavior and little by little you are being captured to support, be neutral or participate as a member of the gay community.

First: The biological sex you have is not determinative. Your real sex is learned and practiced.

Second: The family is above all a decadent religious tradition. The best families are chosen by you according to your sexual preference.

Third: Your sexual behavior is free and can be diverse, according to your self-esteem. Infinite possibilities of manifesting what you can free to do.

Fourth: The conquests of Man towards woman as own and peculiar attitudes of Man like a Gentleman toward a Lady. This ancient men role, they like must be eliminated. Because the men, express aggressiveness, dominance and myogenic attitude.

Fifth: A pregnancy is a legitimate form of oppression that restricts the freedoms of women. On the contrary, freedom of choice, non-commitment and promiscuity guarantee and free women from this commitment. Much more than a Trojan Horse, it is a donkey of the Democrats who imposes on us in a thousand different ways that we accept as good the loss of the Right to Educate our children, that we reject the induction to homosexuality, that sex education is biological and scientific, not following a political agenda to obtain support from the gay community and its followers. To stop all this danger they impose on us, let's learn to say "I do not give up my Right"

Chapter 7

POINT # 5

Huge immigration to destroy identity

THE ENEMY CREATES WAR AND CONFLICT AROUND THE WORLD AND PRODUCES IMMIGRATION STAMPEDE TO EUROPE AND UNITED STATES AND THE IMMIGRANTS ENJOY THE U. S. CONSTITUTIONAL RIGHTS

RESULT: NATIONAL SECURITY AT RISK. The MULTI CULTURAL Factor kills national heritage. OVER CHARGE the Public Services. Demographic Impact. Broken political balances. Increase Unemployment. Fuels CRISIS and Civil War.

1. United States. That's right, ONLY ONE. Every other modern developed nation in the world has gotten rid of birthright citizenship policies.

BIRTHRIGHT CITIZENSHIP POLICY

SOME MODERN COUNTRIES THAT RECENTLY ENDED THEIR BIRTHRIGHT CITIZENSHIP POLICY: Canada was the last non-U.S. Holdout. Illegal aliens stopped getting citizenship for their newborn babies in 2009. Australia's birthright citizenship requirements are much more stringent than those of H.R. 1868 and took effect in 2007.

- New Zealand repealed in 2006.
- Ireland repealed in 2005.
- France repealed in 1993.
- India repealed in 1987.
- United Kingdom repealed in 1983.
- Portugal repealed in 1981.

Groups in conflict around the world create losers or winners for different reasons are induced to abandon their respective countries. This phenomenon has been exploited and, manipulated by the enemy powers. The African continent has had more than 50 years of internal war and severe conflicts; this wave of immigrants has not only invaded Europe but also the United States and South African countries. It is very instructive that immigrants do not take the route of Russia, China, Cuba or North Korea.

The left intellectuals justify with theories such as Coudenhove-Kalergi, which argues that cultural and sociological homogeneity, nullifies the concept of national identity, with the clear objective of creating a more docile society that accepts the rigor of Marxist society.

The 'New European' of Cloward-Piven is also the way to create social and economic collapse to include in the budgets of the State the demands of these groups that lower social productivity.

ILLEGAL IMMIGRANT FEDERAL CONVICTIONS
by 2015
18% OF DRUG TRAFFIC
30% OF KIDNAPING/HOSTAGE TAKING
75% DRUG POSSESSION
10% MONEY LAUNDERING
21% OF NATIONAL DEFENSE
5% OF MURDER
U.S. SENTENCING COMMISSION

The "Multicultural Integration", "American Rainbow", and the "American Pie" concepts baptized with appetizing words, but all of them bring the same result: <u>The Social Suicide of the United States</u>. A new study on immigration highlights that immigration, legal and illegal, increases the population of the United States by 8.3 million every four years.

This immigration has a higher growth rate than the native one and comes precisely from countries hostile to American cultural values. For example, the country Saudi Arabia contributes the largest number of emigrants between the years 2010 to 2014, obtains a growth rate of 93 percent, followed by Bangladesh in 37 percent and in Iraq in 36 percent, while that of the United States is only 1.8% per year.(REF: http://www.wnd.com)

The demographic decrease of Americans, not Hispanics, is 1.8 and is on the way to extinction because the mechanism of filling this population deficit through the granting of visas, and the entry of illegal immigrants lead to the extermination of our own men and women.

It's funny how ecologists protect snakes, wolves, and eagles and other animals in danger of extinction; however, they themselves are in dangerous extinction for more than 30 years and have never raised their voice on this serious issue for the future.

If we analyze which nationalities prevail among legal and illegal immigrants, by their country of origin, we see that there is a common factor among them: In their respective countries, the Immigration Policy is very different. Immigrants are not granted citizenship or labor rights. They do not allow family claims as is usual in the United States.

Social benefits only for US Citizens. The United States need to apply the Reciprocity with foreign citizens are living in the country. How many Americans have received citizenship by naturalization in countries that provide the largest number of legal and illegal immigrants such as Mexico, Cuba, Iraq, Iran, Afghanistan, Turkey, Arab Emirates, Qatar, Somalia, Russia, North Korea, Venezuela, China, India, Iran The account is endless.

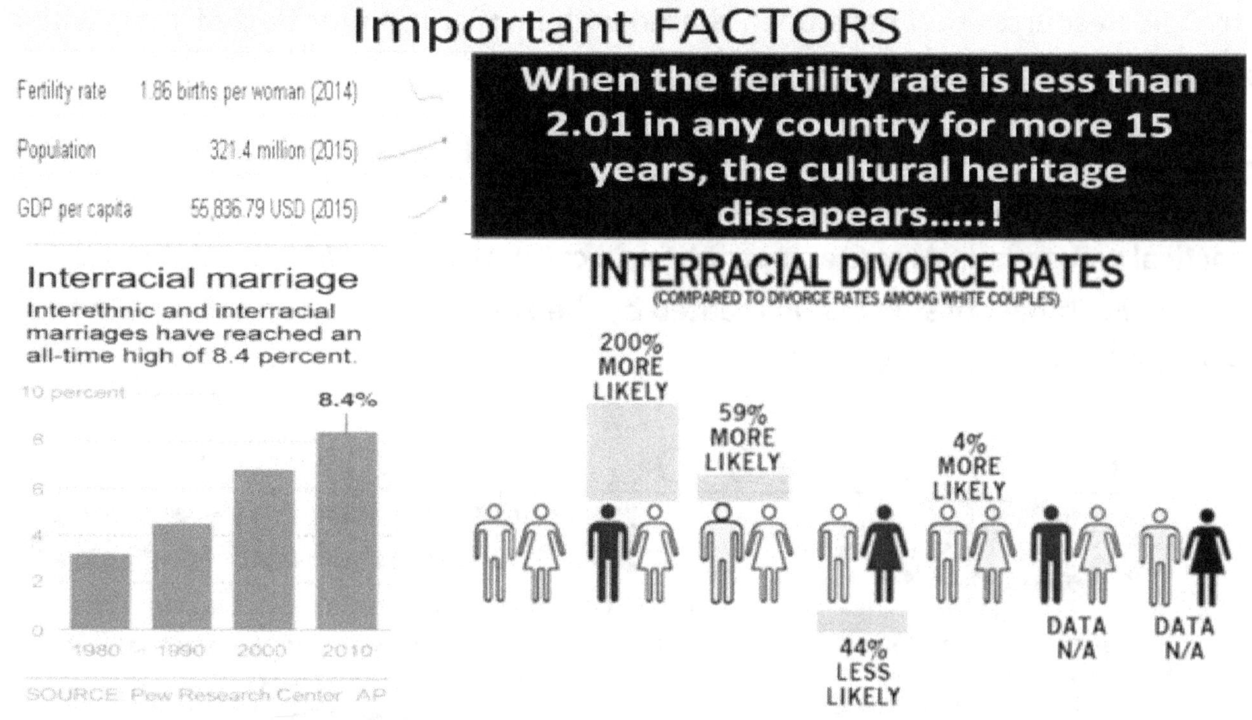

In our days there are   44 million immigrants in the United States they represent 13.5 percent of the population. Worldwide, 1 out of every 5 migrants is in the United States.

The sources of immigration by countries:
Mexico, with 26 %. 1:4 migrants in USA is a Mexican.
India, with 6%
China, with 5%
Philippines, with 4%
El Salvador, Vietnam, and Cuba, each with 3.5%
Dominican Republic, South Korea, and Guatemala, each with 2.5%

The nationals of these 10 countries represent 58% of the total of migrants in the United States. It is opportune that voters facilitate their support to politicians who defend the future of nationals, imposing as do most European countries a tax on descendants of non-national families

COST OF ILLEGAL IMMIGRATION TO AMERICAN TAXPAYERS

$113 BILLION PER YEAR

and that these resources are a function of nationals who have inhibited from having a family due to lack of economic resources, housing, study possibilities, etc. The Resources that have been shared with immigration for tens of years with a cost of billions of dollar every year.

URGENT! If we want to get out of this demographic disaster, the collection of these taxes should be destined to the growing national families. This would be a very practical way to help American patriotic and cultural values prevail and defend against the impact of subversion created by the enemy. This is not a mirage in the desert, it is a concrete reality.

The policy of support for cultural diversity began with local governments or counties. for lack of projection to the future, ignorance, corruption, and liberalism have imposed it, but except our country, cultural diversity is not possible as a banner of war. We are approaching the abyss by the shortest route. Moreover, it is the culminating point to make corruption shine and undermine our culture.

As a historical norm accepted by Humanity for thousands of years, every immigrant arriving in a nation must adapt to the rules and the role it deserves, we must make very clear the idea that immigrants must do what they see, the Bible says. It is necessary where you get to do what you saw ... the immigrants of low cultural level drag the bad or good habits to their new home, to their new sociocultural environment, creating conflicts with the rest of the people and closing the doors to the advantages that can offer you a more advanced society.

Sub-Saharan African, Middle Eastern, and Asian countries saw the largest relative growth in immigrant flows. Immigration from predominantly Muslim countries grew at a rate of 19 percent between 2010 and 2014, including immigration from Saudi Arabia (up 93 percent), Bangladesh (up 37 percent), and Iraq (up 36 percent). Canada and Europe declined as sources of immigration to the U.S.

The analysis comes on the heels of earlier this month showing that a majority (51 percent) of households headed by immigrants used at least one welfare program — such as Medicaid, food aid, housing programs, and cash assistance — significantly higher than the rate of welfare use among native-born–headed households (30 percent). The studies showed that three-fourths of immigrant households using welfare were headed by legal immigrants.— *Mark Antonio Wright is an intern at* National Review.

The US Census Bureau tab 82.18 million American families in the US in 2017, with an average of 3.14 individuals per family nucleus, in 1960 this average was 3.7 people per family. We are condemned to be absorbed by other ethnic groups and cultures, when this same parameter, they reaches an average of 8.9 per family, here in our United States. Demographic Perspective: The Americans in Extinction Process

The Census Bureau forecasts for 2060 prognostic, "One in every three inhabitants in the United States will be of Hispanic origin and Arabs," is currently one in 6 and in 2043 the whites will stop being a majority, according to the 2010 Census. Explained by the interim director of the Census Bureau, Thomas L. Mensenbourg.

This demographic change will have two tendencies: the increase of the Hispanic population, which will go from   53, 3 million to 128.8 million in 2060, and the decline of the white population in total number and in proportion.

The alarming projection of the Census is that there is no real probability that measures will be taken to reduce this disastrous impact and its foreseeable consequences for the development of the country in several aspects.

The natives will grow at a slower pace in the coming decades, compared to the projections made in 2008 and 2009, the levels of births and net international migration are higher, due to the unprecedented fertility and migratory flow, Mensenbourg explained.

Life expectancy increases the population over 65 years of age, which will more than double, in 2060, it will increase from 43.1 million to 92 million, while that of the elderly over 85 years will increase by more than triple, of 5, 9 million to 18.2 million, to reach 4.3% of the population in the country.

In 2043 it will be the United States with most of the population composed of ethnic minorities. In total, all minorities, which now make up 37% of the US population, will be 57% by 2060.

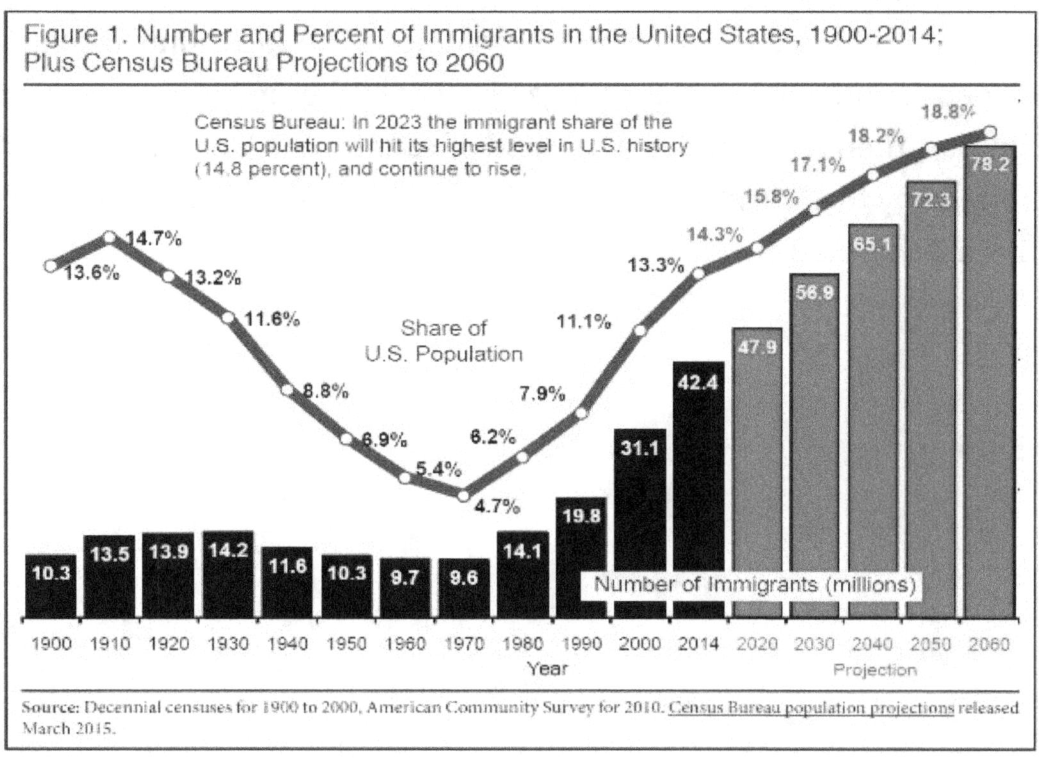

The targets will be only 43%. Hispanics 31%, and blacks 14.7%, the census does not consider the "mestizo" factor; it will decrease significantly to whites. Asians will increase double, from 15.9 million in 2012 to 34.4 million in 2060.   The Pew Research Center. Courtesy

Why do liberals facilitate immigration? Do they know the consequences? Will it leave the United States to be who it is? Why have enemies wiped out the brains of liberals to fight for immigration? Who do they favor? Why do not Russia, China, Iran, Cuba, and North Korea accept immigration?

Immigrants are not significantly patriotic of the United States, do not love, or understand their reasons ... Is this positive for our country?

Usually when a person comes to another country, his psyche automatically makes comparisons with the previous country, with a bit of bewilderment, fear clings to past experiences and tries to maintain their customs, which does not really let him join the new society, but fail to learn because multiculturalism offers to continue with their own habits and customs, each time your frustration will be greater, because it fails to find the necessary accommodation to be similar to the most developed country on the planet. Then he establishes in his life forms were never prosperous, then. We wonder what kind of country the United States will be when it is formed by the "cocktail" or 'pie "of everything has not been winner brings us the State Department.

Chapter #8

The Promotion of excessive drinking and drugs

The drinking-drug taking, the explosion of the 60s "counter-culture," became an even more useful tool of societal and cultural degradation than promoting alcohol-drug abuse - a fact borne out today by continual Leftist attempts to legalize drugs, and pop culture glamorizing drug taking and criminal Subculture.

RESULTING: NATIONAL SECURITY IN RISK. INFECT THE YOUNG PEOPLES. DEMORALIZATION. OVER CHARGE the Public Services. BREAK THE FAMILY. FACILITATE CORRUPTION. INCREASE THE DELINQUENCE. PROSTITUTION. GAMBLING. Fuels CRISIS and Civil War.

Long-term family breakdown, a gateway into criminality, normalization of immoral or self-harming activities - all suit the aims of the Cultural Marxists.

The Cultural Marxist's 'Critical Theories took hold in the tumultuous 1960s, when the Vietnam War opened the Pandora's Box of reevaluation and revolution. The phylospher Herbert Marcuse, a member of the Frankfurt School who preaches the "Great Refusal," a rejection of all basic Western concepts and an embrace of sexual liberation, and the merits of feminist and black revolutions. His first thesis was that university students, ghetto blacks, the alienated, the social, and the Third World, could take the place of the proletariat in the coming communist revolution.

Marcuse may be the most important member of the Frankfurt School in terms of the origins of Political Correctness, because it was the critical link to the counterculture of the 1960s but after the big explosion of addiction of the LSD, cocaine, marihuana, crack, heroin started a new chapter of destruction to our young generation in 1980.

 His main objective was clear: "One can rightly speak of a cultural revolution since the protest is directed towards the whole civilizing establishment, including the morality of existing society but his argument is the justification or the perfect façade to destroy the country.

URSS/Russia, Colombia, Cuba, Mexico and other countries opened their countries to leave free for the maritime route and the airspace for the evil merchandise to reach the United States territory. Source: Drug abuse.gov

This picture is a very representative place, close the town named "Mayari" in the East of the Cuba, you can see in Google map a rare 'square cloud', but under this rare kind of clouds is hidden the Laboratory of the Cuban Armed Forces to produce cocaine in paste.

Castro said in December 1962 in the University of Havana "The Soviet Union came out the nuclear missiles from Cuba, but we have another lethal weapon to destroy the United States; we will offer a lot of shipper drugs to destroy the American society"

 Very early in 1961, Castro ordered to plant millions of eucalyptus trees and bring thousands of people to the municipality of Guane, Pinar del Rio. The planting of millions of eucalyptus trees with the justification of the wind shear curtains. The large curtains of tall eucalyptus were made, but there were no other crops to defend from the winds. It turned out that the eucalyptus is the raw material to produce the LCD (Lysergic Acid) that flooded with its consumption the American youth who was involved in the Vietnam War and on the other hand, to those who convinced if they were not, both used the LCD drug and other at a very low price as Fidel Castro announced in December 1963. Today his intention became truth.

Panoramic View about the Drug Abuse

The main drug used in the teenager is the marihuana. Like a depressant most widely abused is phencyclidine (PCP), AKA angel dust. Inhalants. - Some youths inhale vapors that cause a euphoric feeling that is followed by disorientation, slurred speech, and drowsiness. Like Sedatives and barbiturates to depress the central nervous system, creating a sleeplike condition, tranquilizers, reduce anxiety and promote relaxation: Overuse can lead to addiction, and withdrawal can be painful and hazardous.

Hallucinogens: Provide vivid distortions of the senses without greatly disturbing the viewers consciousness Examples of common hallucinogens: Mescaline, LSD, Stimulants. Synthetic drugs

that increase blood pressure, breathing rate, bodily activity, and elevate mood. Methedrine is the most widely used dangerous amphetamine, aka "meth," "speed," "crystal meth." Economic cost of meth use in the U.S. exceeds $23 billion a year.

Steroids Anabolic steroids are used to gain muscle bulk and strength. Black Market sales approach $1 billion annually. Cause health problems such as liver ailments, tumors, kidney problems, sexual dysfunctions, hypertension and depression Designer Drugs. Some designer drugs are synthetically created in labs for temporarily circumventing existing drug laws (ex: bath salts) Ecstasy: Acts simultaneously as a stimulant and hallucinogen
http://www.youtube.com/watch?v=GS8XY4GMnJk&feature=fvwrel
http://www.youtube.com/watch?v=GS8XY4GMnJk&feature=fvwrel
Cigarettes 40% high school seniors in America have smoked cigarettes in their lifetime. There has been a consistent decline in recent years

As we can understand, the drugs and alcohol addiction is a powerful factor in destroying the individual, the family, and the society, but furthermore, the nation loses billions dollar, with a few results.

Chapter # 9

Point Seven "Empties the Church"

America has been suffering a quiet decline. For the past 40 years, churches have been emptying, and people have turned their backs on God. The impact of this silence against the heavens is tremendous but holds greater influence upon further investigation. The reasons for this trend are multifaceted but can be greatly blamed on two sources. The Schools and the media. Consider that a young child when not at school, spends most of his or her free time-consuming media, and when not consuming media are at school. The substance of these two times an effect views much more risk than imaginable.

This rise in disbelief can be used against us by our greatest enemies. Most if not all, communists of renown were atheists and dreamt of a society without churches. In fact, "about two-thirds of atheists (69%) identify as Democrats (or lean in that direction), and a majority (56%) call themselves political liberals" according to a study conducted by Pew Research Center. This is partially reactionary, due to Republicans being thought of as traditionalists who uphold and impose Christian values, but also due to ignorance of the Bible's teachings. These left-winged atheists support same-sex marriage, abortion, and marijuana usage. Not only are these individuals consuming more and more media to validate their views, but also are most likely the greatest creators of media today. If you take most show's creator, over 50% of the time they are white men who grew up in a Christian or Catholic household and abandoned God. <u>They then pour their views and interests into the arts they create, contaminating a generation of people to think as they do.</u>

 When Yuri Andropov was the head of the Committee for State Security of the Soviet Union, he asked the Academy of Sciences for research on the impact of religion in the history of mankind, the conclusion was very clear when a civilization loses its religion, disappears. The communists place much emphasis on atheism and philosophical materialist approaches.

With the advancement of Science, especially Quantum Physics, Science and Religion merge in a simple and harmonious way, which leaves no room for doubt about the existence of a Divine Intelligence, a Higher Power that is God, our Creator.

Emptying of Church

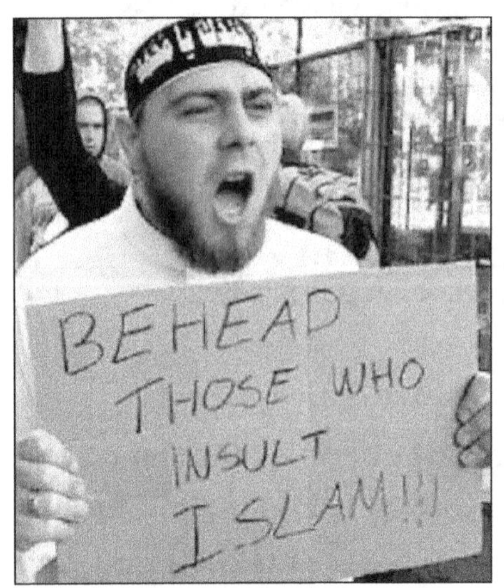

The atheism campaign has been strong against the Judeo-Christianity, but the Muslins have been strong after the September Eleven Increased Attack by the Muslims' Force. This number is a powerful example.

According to a newer estimate done in 2016, there were 3.3 million Muslims living in the United States, About 1% of the total US population. American Muslims from various backgrounds, according to a 2009 Gallup poll, are one of the MOST racially diverse religious groups in the United States.

Reality Is Not Racism, And It Is Not Paranoia When They Are Trying To Kill You.

They do not infiltrate secretly but were officially appointed by a member of the Democratic Party President in the White House. The atheism campaign has been strong against the Judeo-Christianity, but the Muslins' have been increased after the September Eleven Attack by the Muslims' Force. This number is a powerful example.

This map shows the current distribution of Mosques in the United States as of April 2015. This data has been collected from Salatomatic a comprehensive guide to mosques and Islamic schools in the USA. We have in United States 3, 186 mosques in total, California 525, New York 507 and Texas 200, Florida 186, Michigan 139…every year the number is bigger. The Judeo-Christian culture decreased, and the Muslim increased…<u>because we are indifferent, neutral, excessive respect for the foreign behaviors.</u>

The General Igor Shafarevich KGB, one of the directors of this macabre Soviet plan against the West, ordered a study by the Academy of Sciences of the USSR and the Institute of Social Sciences.

<u>He requested a multicultural study to determine the significance of religion in Humanity and found all cultures have passed through the face of the earth have found their collapse and disintegration when they leave the religious concepts initially were why they had joined.</u>

Millions of people have fought, have sacrificed, have remained united with a moral and have eiven their lives for God, by the Faith, but his nemies ,rrepeated:t"Noone has sseen. No one as proven tod, really exists, "however, we all know twice two iarefour, this is an objective truth and no person's life for this truth. Precisely the value of the Faith has made millions of victims throughout history. It is for this reason that Marxism strives to bring atheism to its fullest because once dismissed, the lack of religion destroys a society.

http://www.pewresearch.org/fact-tank/2016/06/01/10-facts-about-atheists/
http://www.pewforum.org/religious-landscape-study/religious-family/atheist/
https://www.quora.com/When-did-atheism-start-to-become-mainstream-and-popular
https://www.quora.com/Why-is-atheism-growing
http://news.nationalgeographic.com/2016/04/160422-atheism-agnostic-secular-nones-rising-religion/
https://www.empty.church/
https://www.theatlantic.com/magazine/archive/2017/04/breaking-faith/517785/

Chapter # 10

An unreliable legal system with bias against the victims of crime

A judicial system aims to complete two goals, punish criminals and protect the innocent. If a judicial system is deemed effective by its citizens, trust in authority is born. What reason is there to fear the police… if you feel they are right and just?

From the subversive perspective, this trust is easily undermined. By giving great media attention to cases involving groups deemed "victims of society," they create a culture that is quicker to point out they are innocent, as the media tells them.   Take, for example, the case of Michael Brown.

POINT # 8

An unreliable legal system with bias against the victims of crime

ALWAYS PROMOTE RESPECT FOR THE PERPETRETOR, IF THE LAW ENFORCE THE ORDER, THEN THE POLICEMAN IS ABUSING.

RESULTING: LACK OF RESPECT TOWARDS AUTHORITY
Because many points of the Frankfort School reinforce the Point # 8 like; The undermining of Schools 'and Teachers' authority. The creation of racist Offenses. Continue change to create confusion. Huge immigration to destroy identity. The promotion of excessive drinking and drugs. Emptying of churches. The minority be impose the majority. CREATE SOCIAL CHAOS!

 A thief who stole a whole box of cigars and pushes aside a clerk to enter his SUV. A cop shot him following the altercation and his noncompliance, leading to a national media war over why this happened. In other words, a thief who resisted and was aggressive towards officers was killed but was only given attention at the national.

level because of his race.

This is one of the many events that led up to the Ferguson Riots, a reaction of the African-American community that stems from misinformation and the identity of "victims" given by the media. This, in turn, causes incredible numbers of not just African-Americans, but all U.S. citizens to distrust police at an alarming rate, and by extension, the justice system.

Chapter # 11

POINT # 9

Dependency on the state or state benefits

UNLIMITED PROTECTION. STOP THE INDIVIVIDUAL INITIATIVE TO BE INDEPENDENT, NO EDUCATION, NO EFFORT TO GET PERSONAL GOALS.

RESULTING: LACK OF PERSONAL MOTIVATION. GET COMPENSATION THE EASY WAY TO REACH LUXURY. EASY MONEY, EASY LIFE, EASY JAIL. AVOID THE EDUCATION IS THE MORE POPULAR ROUTE FOR THE TEENAGER. SPEND THE RETIRED AND DISSABLE BUDGET.

ED PRIDA'S DESIGN

ED PRIDA'S DESIGN

There is a great deal of overlap between resources of welfare dependency and the stereotype of the welfare queen, in that long-term welfare recipients are often seen as draining public resources they have done nothing to earn, as well as stereotyped as doing nothing to improve their situation, choosing to draw benefits when there are alternatives available.

This contributes to the stigmatizing of welfare recipients. While the stereotype of a long-term welfare recipient involves not wanting to work, in reality, a large proportion of welfare recipients is engaged in some form of paid work but still cannot make ends meet.

All of this before the point of view is correct, but the objective of the subversion is to artificially, make the population depend on the government assistance. The totalitarian regime needs to keep the mass absolutely in the hope that the government is the solution to all personal needs. The really healthy way to put in good standing in a country is given the opportunity to produce, sell and purchase according to the power of the main natural and old law of the Offer and the Demand.

The U.S. Congress, U.S. Senate and Federal Government must to abolish the multicultural police at local level, and all type of support the immigration with the sanctuary city, cultural roots, language, and they impose to the nationalities his religions or custom, the Stop is urgent. This not a prejudice, this is not hate, this not discrimination. If we do not open the eyes, we will lost our country.

Chapter # 12

 Control and Dumbing Down of Media

There's a pervasive suspicion of rights, privileges, knowledge, and specialization," says Catherine Liu, the author of American Idyll: Academic Anti-elitist as Cultural Critique and a film and media studies professor at the University of California. The very mission of universities has changed, argues Liu. "We don't educate people anymore. We train them to get jobs."

Part of the reason for the rising anti-intellectualism can be found in the declining state of education in the U.S. compared to other advanced countries:

POINT # 10

Control and dumbing down of media

THE MEDIA CONTROL THE MINDS, DIVIDE THE SOCIETY AND PUT EACH ONE IN FRONT THE OTHER. DISTURBING THE NORMAL DEVELOPMENT.

RESULTING: THE POPULATION BE BRAINWASHING. KEEP THE MASS BLIND, WILD AND FULL OF IGNORANCE. INDIFFERENT. NEUTRAL. FEAR. INSENSIBLE.

SATURATE IGNORANCE. HIDE THE TRUTH. THE HISTORY DISTORTION. SEX IS IN ALL.

ED PRIDA'S DESIGN

After leading the world for decades in 25-34-year-olds with university degrees, the U.S. is now in 12th place. The World Economic Forum ranked the U.S. at 52nd among 139 nations in the quality of its university math and science instruction in 2010. <u>Nearly 50% of all graduate students in the Sciences in the U.S. are foreigners, most of whom are returning to their home countries;</u>

• The Oklahoma Council of Public Affairs <u>commissioned a civic education poll among public school students. A surprising 77% didn't know that George</u>

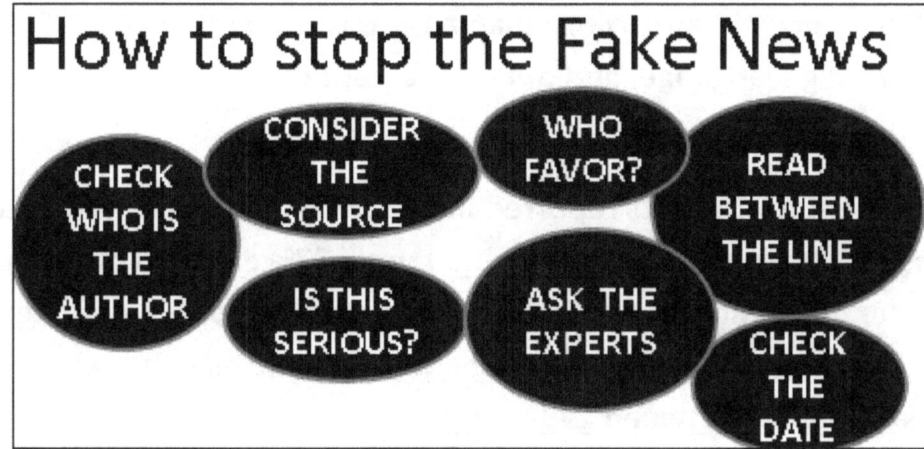

<u>Washington was the first President; It couldn't name Thomas Jefferson as the author of the Declaration of Independence, and 2.8% of the</u> <u>students actually passed the citizenship test. Along similar lines, the Goldwater Institute of Phoenix did the same survey and 3.5% of students passed the civics test;</u>

• _<u>According to the National Research Council report, only 28% of high school science teachers consistently follow the National Research Council guidelines on teaching evolution, and 13% of those teachers explicitly advocate creationism or "intelligent design"</u>_

• 18% of Americans still believe that the sun revolves around the earth, according to a Gallup poll;

• The American Association of State Colleges and Universities reported on education shows that the U.S. ranks second among all nations in the proportion of the population aged 35-64 with a college degree, but 19th in the percentage of those aged 25-34 with an associate or high school diploma, which means that for the first time, the educational attainment of young people will be lower than their parents;

•• <u>The 2009 National Assessment of Educational Progress, 68% of public school children in the U.S. do not read proficiently by the time they finish third grade. And</u>

<u>the U.S. News & World reported that barely 50% of students are ready for college-level reading when they graduate;</u>

- The 2006 survey by National Geographic-Roper, nearly half of Americans between ages 18 and 24 do not think it necessary to know the location of other countries in which news is being made. More than a third consider it "not at all important" to know a foreign language, and only 14 percent consider it "very important"

- The National Endowment for the Arts reported in 1982, 82% of college graduates read novels or poems for pleasure; two decades later, only 67% did. And more than 40% of Americans under 44 did not read a single book--fiction or nonfiction--over the course of a year. <u>The proportion of 17-year-olds who read nothing (unless required by school has doubled between 1984-2004;</u>

- Gallup released a poll indicating 42 percent of Americans still believe God created human beings in their present from less than 10,000 years ago;

- A 2008 University of Texas study found that 25 percent of public school biology teachers believe that humans and dinosaurs inhabited the earth simultaneously.

In American schools, the culture exalts the athlete and good-looking cheerleader. Well-educated and intellectual students are commonly referred to in public schools and the media as "nerds," "dweebs," "dorks," and "geeks," and are relentlessly harassed and even assaulted by the more popular "jocks" for openly displaying any intellect. These anti-intellectual attitudes are not reflected in

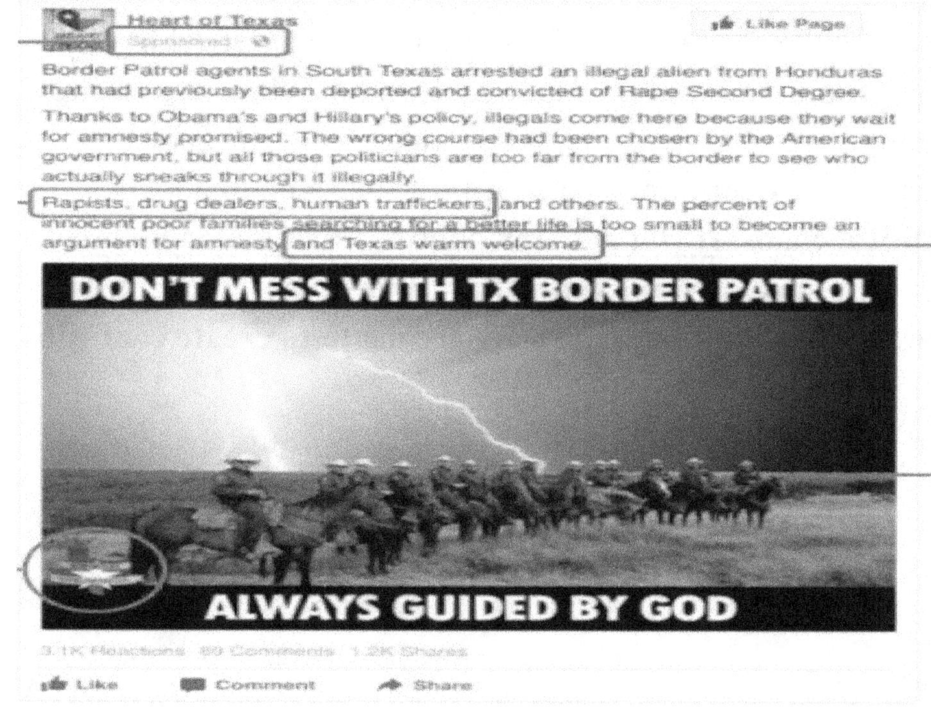

students in most European or Asian countries, whose educational levels have now equaled and will surpass that of the U.S., And most TV shows or movies such as The Big-Bang Theory depict intellectuals as being geeks if not effeminate.

With this shortening of attention span, the modern man is far more open to deception and misinformation by the media at large. Scandalous, inflammatory headlines are the only thing a shocking number of our population has time for.

They take these bits and pieces fed to them and believe them. This is what George Orwell feared. "A nation of sheep ruled by wolves."

Subversion from Russia and Cuba

A raw instance of subversion can be found here. Troll farms are groups of computer-savvy individuals funded by the Russian and Cuban government to divide America politically using social media. Ads are created for the sole purpose of polarizing the reader into a strong right-wing stance or equally left stance. The effect of this is to stir up controversy and inflammatory comments in the minds of US citizens.

The Commander of the Revolution Ramiro Values Menendez, two times Minister of Interior is in charge of a new Minister, called Informatica.

This Ministry of Informatics has hundred of Computer Engineer checking the Media, Hacking, and writing inflammatory and aggressive opinions against any manifestation in favor to fix our problems.   Further solidifying the growing notion of a problematic and this-conjoined America for the sole purpose of creating only more political chaos. <u>If you had any doubt in subversion before, this is nothing less than raw proof.</u> At the times, they write down the names of prominent personalities or individual who already are death to create confusion between the groups of people.

Chapter # 13

Point Eleven Encouraging the breakdown of the Family

The family is a symbol, base of the main cell of society. To dismiss the family role, status and rules is an involution like a society fundamental brick, where every member does not have an identity, and neither had an orientation.

POINT # 11

Encouraging the breakdown of the family

THE CULTURAL MARXISM TARGETED THE FAMILY FROM DIFFERENT SIDES BECAUSE THIS SOCIETY IS FOUNDED UPON THEM.

RESULTING: BROKEN AUTHORITY OF PARENTS AND TEACHERS, SEEDING FALSE EXPECTATION, ABORTION, ATHEISM, TEACHING AND INDUCTING THE HOMOSEXUALITY, BROKEN CULTURAL HERITAGE WITH HUGE IMMIGRATION AND MULTICULTURAL ISSUES AND FREE SEX THE FAMILY TENDENCY IS TO THE DESINTEGRATION...

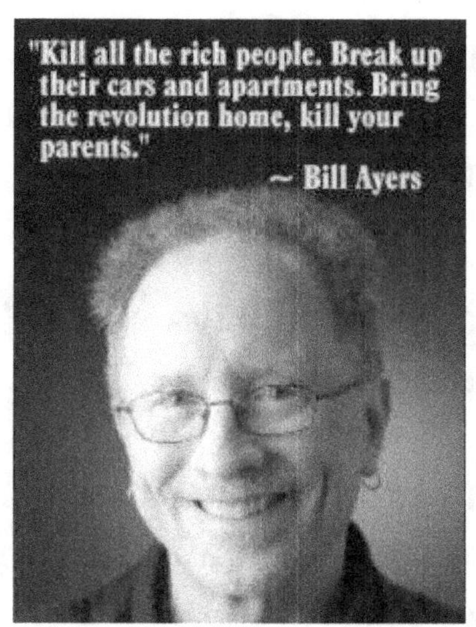

The free sex, the abolition of the legal married and establishing a modern kind of couples without civil responsibilities with the children, neither the mother, neither the father, housing, feed, education, spiritual guideline, clothes, shoes, medical and dental assistance. Probably the brand new generation raised under this condition will be very close to being a wild person. This destructive factor is a perfect element to be driven by a totalitarian regime.

Barack Obama and Bill Ayers in the same mission, destroy our society, our family, and our country.

Some define a family purely in terms of a group of peoples who living in the same household together. Others define the family based on kinship. A family is a group of people who share common ancestors or genetic heritage, and the primary social unit composed of parents and their children. The family is a kind of "Holy Concept," the family is the primary structure of the society. The family grows and transmitted the cultural heritage and the better social values.

 The biological kinship is the defining element of family, while opponents assert that families can be a blended collection of individuals related by marriage, adoption, partnership, or friendship.

The most eloquent picture I saw in my life. You can get your conclusion.

Every culture put a seal in the peculiarities of the family way to get every goal to accomplish the grow of the newborn and elder member. Each religion gives roles, status, and laws to get the supreme goals.

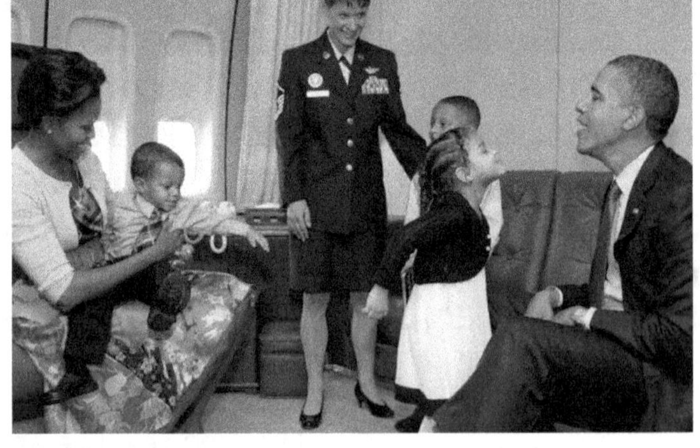

Social theorists have questioned the nature of family since the ancient times. In the last century has witnessed transformations of prevailing concepts of family according to the different cultures. The African Continent is the ground of thousands of tribes with structure roles, norms, and status for each member of the family group.

The Western society, in general, the family is a comprehensive social unit formed by physical, biological, emotional, and economic necessities. Every couple can choose the partner Freeling in few cases of married is mandatory like in Africa or Asia. The external and internal dynamic in the human group makes many changes that can affect every member in the different manner of families through divorce and remarriage. Furthermore, provided herein is demographic information on what contemporary families and households look like in the United States.

The family, the herd, the couple has a common goal, grow the newborn giving care, food, housing, and protection.

 How individuals conceptualize the family is influenced by culture, religion, law, and politics. We have a bound by blood, the children of incarcerated parents. The 54% of the male in prison are parents with children, including more than 120,000 mothers and 1,3 million parents. One in every 28 children has a parent in prison. A total of 2,7 million children involved in his parents in prison, the increased up from half of million in 1980 of children.

Abortion has killed over 58 million American baby citizens in our beloved nation since 1973. Planned Parenthood is killing over 320,000 innocent, unborn Americans in the womb in our country every year....

The family is weak, because the father or/and the mother can be disappearing, and the family receive an impact and need to be restructured to continue with the support of the children.

<u>The main force of the subversion long-term plan is destroying the family</u> by the different manner. Without authority to respect, not order, no religion, and in another hand the free sex, drugs. They get the short cut to delinquent behavior, economic dependency, lack opportunity to study, many expectations and few result create the frustration, inconsistency in the purpose, etc.

When the family is broken the State took the control of the child and molding his/her or her mind, without family love and moral heritage. The group will modeling the personality and moral rule.

This kind of citizen has very high probability to go to the jail or a ruin life. Impact of the new model of the Family Dynamic: a Result of Lack of Family Attention.

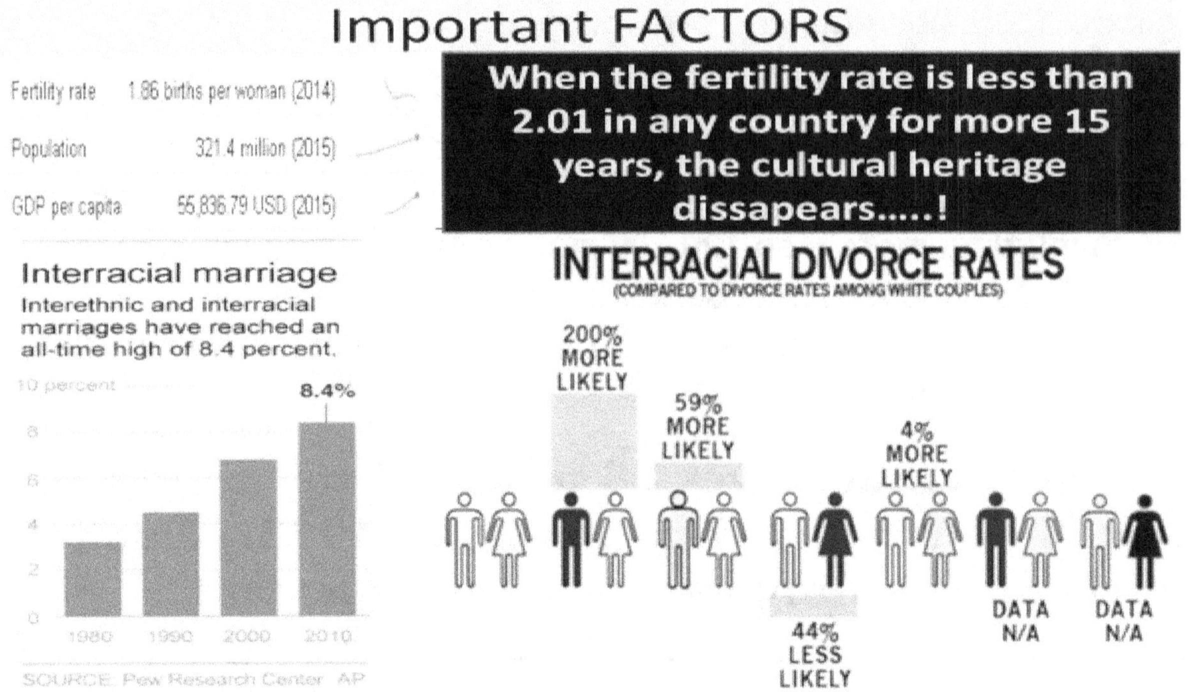

Like the results, the subversive culture we have is a unknown type family structure with a irregular role, status, and rules that have been changing for everyone. To understand why, take in account, the first cause of 90% of suicidal behavior is the consequence of bad or lack relationship with the family, especially... the lack of affection and close relationship.

The increased suicide rate in people aged between 10 and 24 years, increased by 13%, in 2014 and the figure reached 5504 youth suicide deaths. This is sad.

Pay attention, it´s the second-leading cause of death for those aged 10 to 24. By comparison, suicide is the 11th leading cause of death for all those age 10 and over, with 33,289 suicides for all US citizens in 2006.

According to the Center for Disease Control and Prevention (CDC), suicide is considered the second leading cause of death among college students, the second-leading cause of death for people ages 25–34, and the fourth leading cause of death for adults between the ages of 18 and 65.

In 2015, the CDC also stated that an estimated 9.3 million adults, which is roughly 4% of the United States population, had suicidal thoughts in one year alone. 1.3 million adults 18 and older attempted suicide in one year, with 1.1 million making plans to commit suicide.

Closely watching of teenagers, suicide is the third-leading cause of individuals aged from 10 to 14. Males and females are known to have different suicidal tendencies. For example, males take their lives almost four times the rate females do. Males also commit approximately 77.9% of all suicides. However, the female population is more likely to have thoughts of suicide than males. Males more prevalently use a firearm to commit suicide, while females generally use a form of poison. College students aged 18–22 are less likely to attempt to suicide than teenagers.

In 2013, at national level, a total of 494,169 people were treated in emergency departments for self-inflicted, nonfatal injuries, which left $10.4 billion in combined medical and work loss costs.

Female Suicide Rates by Race

Suicide rates vary for ethnic groups due to cultural peculiarities. In 1998, suicides among European Americans accounted for 84% of all youth suicides, 61% male, and 23% female. However, the suicide rate for Native Americans was 19.3 per 100,000, much higher than the overall rate (8.5 per 100, 000).). The suicide rate for African Americans has increased more than two-fold since 1981. A national survey of high-school students conducted in 1999 showed the Hispanic students were twice as likely attempted suicide than white students.

LGBT

Researchers have found that suicide among lesbian, gay, bisexual, trans gender (LGBT) youth is comparatively higher than among the general population. LGBT teens and young adults have one of the highest rates of suicide attempts.

Alcohol, Drug Abuse, Depression, Frustration by the abnormal behavior standard in the family, social group and any institutions for working, military, study, churches, they receive the adaptation answer, because they damage the family and the society.

Causes of teenage suicide

Teenage suicide is not caused by any one factor, but likely by a combination of them. Depression can play a massive role in teenage suicide. Some contributing 18 factors, but 90 % of the main cause is the lack of a relationship with of the parents.

 Eating disorders have the highest correlation with suicide in 15% because it is perceived as a lack of parental interest, and it is also a major factor in teenage suicide. According to one study, 90% of suicidal teenagers believed their families did not understand them.

Depression is the most common cause of suicide. About 75% of those individuals who commit suicide are depressed. Depression is caused by some factors, from chemical imbalances to psychological make-up to environmental influences.

If we know that those social events have been a plan of our enemies internal and external, we can give solutions.

Ref:

Author archives

https://www.encyclopedia.com/social-sciences/applied-and-social-sciences-magazines/introduction-concepts-family

Chapter # 14

KGB's Subversion Plan against the United States.

The Soviet leadership replaced Nikita because their plans were unsuccessful. He was followed by General Leonid Brezhnev, who had long been charged with directing the production of nuclear devices to attack the United States.

He instituted the so-called Brezhnev's Doctrine, which planned the same attack; but, in the longer term, to have more time to perfect the production of nuclear deliveries; Since they knew that those who had developed it, did not have the efficiency required for the assigned mission. Brezhnev is carrying out his plan, even though it has been in operation since the 1960s with Operation Bridgehead, the second consecutive operation of the KGB from Cuba against the United States. (For more information, see the Sovietization of Cuba and its Consequences by the same author.)

In 1980, Yuri Andropov, head of the State Committee for State Security of the USSR and his group of social scientists from the USSR Academy of Sciences outlined a plan based on the old scheme always used by the Soviets to destroy a target nation); And, starting from what was devised, began a project of political subversion against the United States.

"America is like a healthy body and resistance is threefold: It's patriotism; It's morality, and its spiritual life. If we can undermine these three, America will collapse from within" Joseph Stalin.

This second Plan to subvert the order in the United States was born because the USSR had, in a certain way, given up its economic and industrial superiority, and therefore, military, as Nikita Khrushchev had thought through his hypocritical policy of Emulation and Peaceful Coexistence. This attempt now seemed feasible to have Cuba as a base to the south of the United States from where they could attack efficiently and destroy America, in more ways than one. The passing of time proved that the USSR could never have achieved, as it did, the scientific and military development achieved by the United States.

"Bravo Operation" Cuba/KGB

In 1980, this plan was implemented, making maskirovka (mask) the crisis of the Embassy of Peru, in Cuba, taking advantage of the death of a member of the Police who died because of a shot in the back by the other policeman on duty at this location.

The public scene: A group of social no adapted citizens penetrated with their families in the Embassy of Peru in Miramar. May 1980

Applying an active measure, Castro handled an "incident by induction "to turn it into a rush against US using humans. He announced that anyone who wished to leave the Island could do so. The Cubans took the chance, and this incident made it possible for hundreds of thousands of people to try to penetrate the Peru's embassy, and then started the Mariel´s Exodus in May 1980.

In fact, two years ago before, in 1978, the Directorate of Biological War of the Ministry of Defense of the USSR, specifically called "BioPreparad" under the direction of a doctor named Ken Alibek. He had been ready to use, the virus that we had now known as HIV, but was not used to install it aboard intercontinental missiles because it was not effective enough to kill in less than 15 days, as required by Ministry of Defense standards.

According to Dr. Ken Alibek, this virus, which they had developed so painstakingly, passed it on to the Special Operations of the KGB, to be used in local conflicts as part of the psychological warfare that the URRS carried out around the world. The Soviets transformed into weapon biological warfare pathogenic viruses obtained in Africa where they exist endemic and epidemic. Today is known as the HIV and became thus a reserve weapon for future use.

It should be clarified that this was not the way that HIV reached the population of Cuba. Cuba did not create a "sanitary and epidemiological barrier" to detect diseases among the Castro/Russian mercenaries returning from Angola. All went directly to their homes transmitting, infected, AIDS and other diseases to their women through sexual intercourse and to their children.

* Author's Note: During the Mariel Exodus, the KGB, operating from Cuba, created the propitious opportunity to Introduce Hiv in the United States. Personally, I saw the Soviet doctors vaccinate patients at the National Psychiatric Hospital and prisoners who served long sentences for common crimes such as robbery, murder, rape, etc. Which the Cuban government sent through the port of Mariel between April and May 1980. Furthermore, the Doctor Ken Alibek, who was the Director of Bio, prepared the Soviet Empire producer of biological weapons, in his book Biohazard, he describes that they designed the HIV to use in onboard of the ICBM, but the Department of Defense required killing the enemies within 15 days. This is the reason that this kind of weapons was used by the Psychological Operation in the hands of KGB, like in Cuba in 1980.

Years later, as a political prisoner, I met in Quivican prison, many prisoners who had been sent by the Cuban Government to the United States in 1980, and who were later repatriated to the island for their criminal behavior in American territory. These explained to me, in detail, what their missions had been in the prisons of the United States.

Also, it was another task to have demoralized, in the eyes of the press and the general population, the good people who left the country in search of a nation that respected the human and civil rights that had been given to them, but denied in Cuba. Logically, the personalities, his peculiar body language, and behavior of those inmates who for more than 15 or 20 years had been subjected to the system of prisons, caused a terrible impression in the Media.

The impact in the prisons where they was concentrated changed the rules between the inmates forever. They committed and the taught brand new kinds of crimes, how to produce alcohol, drugs, ink for tattoo, weapons hand make, and other. These skills increased the corruption between the prison authorities, the drug production mixing medication. These prisoners and his crimes were taken by the press as a representative of person who wanted to leave Cuba because they were dissatisfied with the social organization that the Castro-Communist system offered its citizens. Some leftish journalist published these events against the Cuban exile's reputation

Why introduce a disease in another country?

In the contemporary world, this phenomenon has a very counterproductive appearance and is only conceivable within the inhuman and cruel ideology, bizarre attitude.

The Plan started in 1975; the Castro's regime increased the prison population with the Law Number 59. Just in Havana, got like prisoners 60,000 male and 13,000 young women in prison. The KGB ordered a reserve population in prison to send to United States like a passive invasion of 120,000 persons. There are dangerous criminals and psychiatrics inmates between them for thousands. The main target, create problem and conflict in United States.

The criminals and psychiatric patient were detected and went to prison, just arriving to United States. They introduced aggressive behaviors and the HIV like a bioweapons in every prison; A new disease attacked the inmates population, the Center for Diseases Control detected the transmission by sexual contact between prisoners. Everybody understood the disease is just transferred by gays. While, some celebrities started with Sarcomas and other cancers as consequence of the HIV. The Medical Science learned that the virus can infest any person by the heterosexual intercourse, too.

But he KGB's Plan "Bravo" in 1980 opened the gate of the "homosexual behavior" because celebrities and famous sportsman got the virus. The outbreak called the attention and leave a powerful message: "Terror, Demoralization, Billion dollars of cost, but furthermore the homosexual activities was alive in the closet".

The Josef Stalin's idea to destroy morally the United States became true.   The introduction of Cuban prisoners who were carriers of a sexually transmitted disease, were intended to graft a "prison culture" with which they could increase corruption and create an internal crisis in prisons; and knowing that the main mechanism of learning is imitation, they thought that in the next 20 or 30 years, these behaviors could contaminate other segments of the general population, because as we know the prison population behaves as the population of the patients of a hospital institution or a hotel.

A third of the prison population have a long stay, and the other 2/3 are renewed more frequently; this recycling of the population could be the carriers of "prison" behavior to the outside society of the prison.

The contaminating population imposed fresh forms of leadership in the internal gangs. They had the form to manufacture hallucinogenic drugs with the medication, also the elaboration of drinks with high alcohol content just with sugar and fruits. The well-known homosexual activity took a modern turn of violence, typical of the prison population exported by Cuba, but more corrupt with a deadly sexually transmitted disease, which could create, as indeed it did, astronomical losses to the government of the United States. They would bring with it a new appraisal of the concept of "manhood" in the scale of moral values of American society, fulfilling one of the primary objectives of political and ideological subversion in its first phase of demoralization.

On the other hand, the rebelliousness, daring, and mischief of the Cuban prisoners would serve to quickly contaminate the American prison population. It instituted the tattoos in full scale, the most sophisticated evasion inventions, corruption of the police and the administration involving them in the export of the drugs to the outside of the prisons.

New ways to impose leadership by a closed group were left unanswered. American criminals in their courtyard became visitors with their mechanisms to first recruit to their group, the police and administrators, first selling information and then with becoming commodities in very lucrative business.

Many of the Cuban prisoners who had been prepared for this event, in some cases abducted criminal authorities taking advantage of the relations they had already established with the heads of the prison institutions themselves and provoked revolts, hunger strikes, fires, etc., as it happened in a prison in the state of Georgia and in other American prisons. The Presdient Ronald Reagan sent the Ambassador Armando Valladares like a mediator, and resolved the problem.

This active measure of sending the prisoners is woven into the changes become of the psycho-social phenomena and were taking body in the United States society by the impact of the changes and efforts of the American nation in the Second World War, of which, among other factors transformed the so-called "family dynamics" with the incorporation of women to work to supply the men who had gone to war and then the recomposition of the family in some cases in an absence by death and in others by the replacement of the head of the family, so the concept of role or role played by the traditional mother disappeared from the homes in the 40s by incorporating to work in manufacturing industry, each renewed role generated norms of behavior, and leadership now fostered certain conflicts did not exist before.

The Subversion Process

  Demoralization consists in operating a change in the perception of the social and political phenomena that prevail in the environment where the individuals of a country or a geographical region operate. In other words, it is creating the conditions for people to modify and develop attitudes or opinions contrary to those they had before.

When we are neutral, permissive or tolerant with all the proposals of the enemy, we lose this battle, the enemy wins this battle easily; With this attitude, we do not have a behavior of permanent and active opposition, and from the start, the enemy has conquered. Making ourselves neutral is the number one goal of the Psychological War, through "demonstrating" that corruption exists.

Communists can achieve the goal, over a period of about 15 to 20 years; It suffices to expose the ideas professed by the enemy to successive generations, destroying the frameworks of moral and psychological reference. To point out that there is something beyond the imaginative reach of the individual who could be much better than what he knows, creates motivational and cognitive tension, what we know as "Curiosity" in the citizen.

These Muslim leaders inside the White House, they are not moles, neither infiltrated foreign agents; President Barack Obama assigned them.

Recall that the silent "majority" as he said, I see the current President Donald Trump (the Comodin selected by the Universe to resolve the conflicts of our Mother-Earth).

 It is not easy to find in history an emerging leadership of the majorities, and that leads them to the fight against minorities. The opposite, it was used by Vladimir Lenin to create communist partisans being always infamous minorities. A Marxist Party is one of a tiny minority to drag the masses at their convenience. This is what happened in Japan with the Japanese militarists, as is the case with Islamic extremists, a minority is capable of killing and sowing terror, whereas a large majority of Muslims may not be extremists like their leaders, but they remain passive, waiting for victory. Take advantage of the victory. Image

They propitiate insecurity, through terrorism, economic chaos, unemployment, rising commodity prices due to induced shortages, the real estate crisis, actively and deliberately create events to manipulate them to your interest.

A Russian Tu-95 Bear H. (Associated Press) ** FILE ** A Russian Tu-95 Bear H. (Associated Press) * To mention but a few examples of demoralization we can cite: hoisting the Mexican flag in school institutions in California; The assassination of President Kennedy; Establishing a chair of Marxist philosophy in a teaching institution and creating a fan club of Lenin or Che Guevara.

The airspace violations by Russian TU-95 for 16 times in 10 days. December 2014 over the airspace of Alaska and California but on July 4th. They flew over the Gulf of

Mexico and Louisiana territory several times; those bombers take off from San Antonio Air Force Base in Cuba.

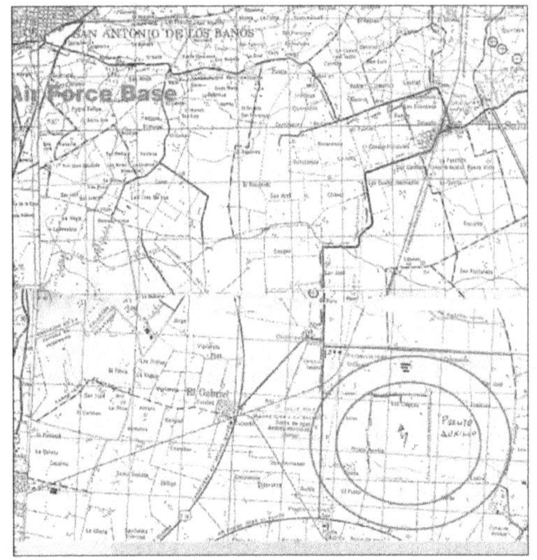

The Russia Armed Forces have the air base in Cuba with strategic bombers Tupolev Tu-195, missiles SS-22, Saturn Naval Missiles, base for nuclear submarines in Cienfuegos's Port, Container Base with Medium-Range Missiles hidden inside in Mariel Bay, Center for Wheather Modification (code Pronto Auxilio)in Guira de Melena and multiple Electronic Surveillance bases, Intelligence advisers and interchange information and tasks with Russia, China, Iran and North Korea.

Demoralization whose function begins to devalue, to disenchant the average citizen of the pillars supporting their society.

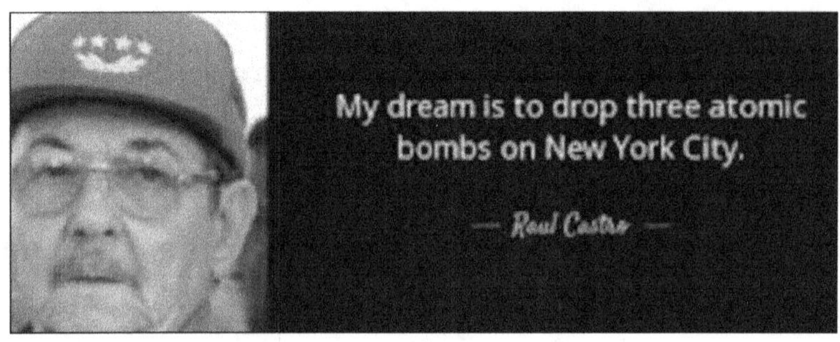

They undermine the prestige of an army attacking a military garrison by surprise and then with the help of the press, exaggerating the defense response against the perpetrators of the fact as if they were tortured; make emerge an opposition leader denouncing alleged corruption or not fair, and proposes new measures to amend problems that exist or may not exist, just to make people lose confidence in the institutions that should be pillars of the state.

Examples of ideological subversion in the United States used to attack "Dark of the CIA and", "Witch Hunter FBI", "Fake Moon landings by NASA", publishing news coming out of the workshops of intelligence agency's enemy or undermine the prestige of religion to the spread of information about the lewd activity of priests. The Twin Tower attack leave four thousand innocent worker's death and billions of dollars in damages...9/11 Never forgetter.

Every act of terrorism is for the demoralization of our public defensive institution.

These examples are one of the ways to create gradually, neutrality in concepts previously defended, or otherwise, which irritated and cursed us before, we now see it without any reaction. To become neutral is when the enemy has already taken us completely.

Its success lies in penetrating our minds, our values, of whatever nature it may be, and get to see or otherwise expose us not to react; and even get people who have come to say, "I respect them."

The core dragging society toward the enemy is made up of social misfits, nonconformists, the enemies of personal sacrifice for improvements, psychopaths and sociopaths. These elements, enemy agents group them so that giving support to push their ideas and using different institutions give them prestige and importance as public figures.

This picture, with a white baby girl with a black doll in the hands, in a few hours, was seen on social networks for a quarter of a million people, simply because they claimed that we were not born with racial preferences.

However, the biological reality laid by our Creator, all species have a mechanism called "Specificity of the Substrate "consisting of hormones secreted by the penis into the uterus which carry a genetic code for the egg, appears from the body but has the same species, because otherwise they could create random chaos, in the development of species. in other ways, these hormones and their genetic code are not similar and can support uterine cancer.

This is an example of the interest of the enemy by mixing the races using propaganda to increase interracial couples, this phenomenon we have seen as a common factor where they want to plant subversive Marxist ideas by any means necessary.

 The desired results with this monstrosity are to create divisions at all levels by inducing conflicts of interest between couples, families, and children also change the demographic structure of a nation, and its cultural degeneration rigged.

While ELP press characterizes them as leaders, they give legitimacy to expose the reasons for charging with respect and strength; therefore, more and more people join or are active in these groups. The KGB has used a pattern to select leaders based primarily on choosing those who are distinguished by their ability to lie and make promises, for their indolence and possessing a pathological egocentricity.

This stage centralizes its activities in the areas of the economy, the family and the armed forces.

Other factors, while not falling into these categories, specifically, may be useful also to subversive dissidents. Additionally, many tools may overlap into other groups of tools as well. As an example, subversives may infiltrate an organization for culture, more so than for subversion control. Civil Unrest may be used to provoke the government into a violent response.

Infiltration and Establishing Front Groups

For a group to be successful in subverting a government, the group itself and its ¨Ideas¨ must be an acceptable alternative to the status quo.

They need to mask the true purpose of the organization with other names and "objectives," and then a link needs to the solution those that this ideology can provide. This was a way that the Communist Party USA controlled many different organizations, such as the Democratic Party, the Muslins, the House of Maryland and many more, organized in the United States.

These groups that work toward subverting a government, in many cases, follow ideals and promote their surface on goals that would not receive the support of the population.

Therefore, "to gain public credibility and attract new supporters, generate revenues, and acquire other resources, these groups need to undertake political activities that are entirely unconnected or appear unrelated, from the overtly violent activities of those groups. Sometimes this is achieved by infiltrating political parties, labor unions, community groups, and charitable organizations ". Infiltrating organizations is an important tool because these Institutions are already seen as legitimate in the eyes of the people and express provide a platform for their ideas.

When infiltrating, the dissident identifies and employs. Once the organization has been operational co-opt, then the dissident can move on to other groups to establish ties with.

Furthermore, in addition to gaining legitimacy for possible infiltration of the thoughts, it´s these groups that can, "bolster political allies, attack government policies, and attract International support." If some are organizations, too difficult to infiltrate, it may be necessary to create new institutions that appear to be independent but are under the direction of the subversive group. For example, the 26th of July Movement was under design and control of the KGB; House of Maryland was under control of the United States Communist Party.

The infiltration of State Department: Organizations can provide to subversive groups the opportunity to do many things to achieve their goals.

The infiltration of security forces, CIA and FBI and other Agencies (Intelligence's Community) Provide information that can tell about the government's capabilities and how to drive his plans. <u>Is important to know, our enemies work for long term goals and they are in offensive mode all the time.</u>

Infiltration also provides the opportunity to plant false information, leading the government to dislocate resources, to steal funds, weapons, equipment, and other resources, and aid in weakening and ultimately from illegitimating the government. The targets of infiltration are not limited to the groups and institutions mentioned above. The manufacturing, education, publisher, mass media, commerce, transport, powers, and the hard sciences.

 For one Precautionary Measure that could assume any group, organization, or institution that may help sway the review and beliefs of the citizenry against the government could be a target for infiltration.

Economics

Economics can be a tool. Both internal and external subversive method. For the external subversive, cutting off credit simply can cause severe economic problems for a country. An example of this is the United States' relations with China; we have a complete dependency on internal consumer marketing. The main objective of economic pressures is to make it difficult for the country to Fulfill Obligations to the basic citizenry by cutting off trade or by depriving it of resources.

The internal subversive also can use economics to put pressure on the government through the strike and revolt.

But, the economic block is just a symbolic or fictitious action, because the totalitarian regimes need the misery to keep political control over every individual, that is the reason to implant the socialist society. They need to create an artificial crisis on the food, water, transport, medical service, etc. They need to create a total dependency on the regime.

Public Agitation

Provocative action receives the defensive action by creating public order force and the victim's role, and these cases are the target of the leftist journalist, calling the attention to get new members for the cause.

These tools demonstrate the need to further determine the intent of taking action to identify those subversive activities.

Civil unrest creates many of the problems that an insurgency campaign does. First of all, it is an affront and challenges to government authority, and if the government is unable to quell the unrest, it leads to an erosion of state power. This loss of power stems from the people's lack of trust in the government to maintain law and order. In turn, the people begin to question whether new leadership is needed. Afterward, they use the victims to get support.

Discrediting, disarming, and demoralizing the government is the goal of these activities and the cause of the government's loss of power. Civil unrest depletes resources as the government is forced to spend more money on additional police.

Additionally, civil unrest may be used to provoke a response from the government. In the 1940s communists in France During strikes against the Marshall Plan would, "deliberately provoke the police and gendarmerie into acts of violence to repress, ¨then exploit the RESULTING martyrs to the cause for propaganda purposes."

These martyrs and subsequent advertising can be useful in turning political and social groups against each other. The less violent forms of unrest, such as "worker absenteeism," passive resistance, boycotts, and deliberate attempts to cripple government agencies by" overloading the system 'with false reports, can have powerful disruptive effects, both economic and politically."

The US had always been a conservative country, since the late 50´s, movements began to arise, rejection of certain groups, respected in society with the support of the (left) liberals and the press in search of selling product values with new computer contents that attract attention and break the rules.

The banks appear at this time, the conservative form of life opposed and sought to promote the concepts of materialism. This was led by artists who also used drugs, dressed in a peculiar way and led a dissolute life, sexually motivated. In the 60s, the hippies, who openly promiscuously used marijuana and lived in communes, in total rebellion against the conservative habits of the American people emerge. Furthermore, in this decade, prayer and mention of God in schools by claims of atheistic movements, it is suppressed.

As we see all these elements were supported by the media and the performing arts as part of subversion.

Seeking justice, equal rights movement of the black minority makes another impact on American society. The women's liberation movement brings changes to the behavior of many women who express their thinking getting dressed without underwear, rejecting marriage in favor of coexistence, supporting abortion, etc. The Homosexuals are gaining ground to be accepted despite their sexual preferences; and openly, many celebrities begin to show their way of life publicly. Everything that happened on par protests against the war in Vietnam.

All these factors were covertly exploited to demoralize around the planet the United States, for much institution's appearance of being independent of the USSR but were created and supported by intelligence agencies and diplomatic means of the socialist camp in general.

Students in the 70s, in many universities, expressed their rebellion against the puritanical traditions of the American people, wandering around the grounds´ mass of institutions, with nonchalance, and sometimes completely naked in fleeting demonstrations by university gardens. Lightning demonstrations were rarely, by the speed with which it took place; police could never stop it.

It is the time of "do your own thing" in this society.

American life as it was known began to acquire other characteristics. At the end of the 70s and during the 80s was the time of the proliferation of drug mafias, mainly Colombian and Castro / Cubans in US territory; to which many of these were prepared and sent via the Mariel by the Castro government individuals who were incorporated. Certainly, in the cities where these criminal groups concentrated were a contributing factor to break with crime and illicit communities that hosted activities.

Psychotropic Drugs prepared in prisons from mixing different kinds of medication, men with long hair, without hygienic care, illegal alcoholic beverages from fruits and sugar, became a business with the jailers, leadership gangs and administrative corruption in prisons was the legacy left by these offenders in American prisons. No doubt some of those who did not go to prison, but they were coming, and they are still coming, as infiltrator's part of that mission, in some US cities has also been a factor of social decomposition.

A striking example is the large number of Cubans trained in Cuba to create Medicaid fraud that has made Miami the capital of this kind of crime, as well as getting easy money and dirty clique of Cuba; this demoralization generates and creates a bad reputation for Cuban exiles.

The So-Called Counterculture in America manifests social level emblematic behaviors that make them stand out for the use of absurd and bizarre behavior's clothes, hats backward, tattoos, pants in odd sizes and below the waist.

 Those who adopt this "lifestyle" project as well as in the field of exercise of their civil and political rights. When cared is apathetic to the general objectives of society individuals who do not participate in elections and lose interest in civic duties to be fulfilled by not joining the organs of national defense since that compulsory military service was abolished. These plans usually consume an approximate time of one or two generations to achieve tangible results and once established are impossible to amend.

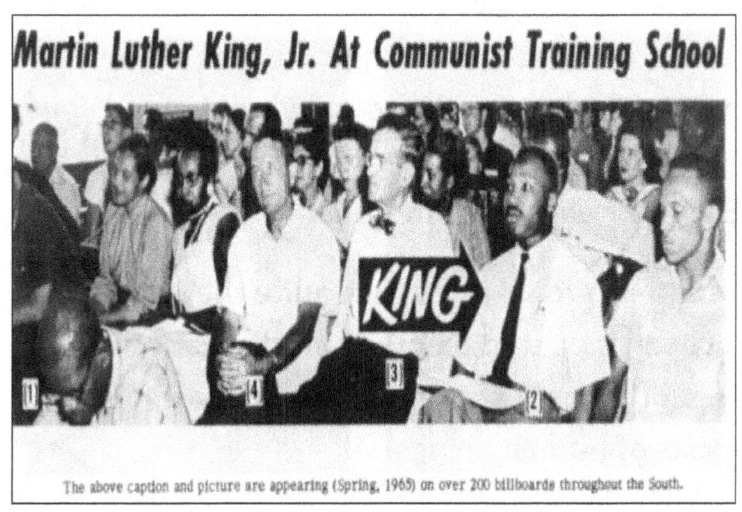

The above caption and picture are appearing (Spring, 1965) on over 200 billboards throughout the South.

This kind of social destruction has many advantages over the classic war on the battlefield because it uses the extensive freedom and rights of citizens who facilitate by the Constitution of the United States and their legal bodies, moving beyond the limits of state institutions.

They have to track down and control the ideas and actions contrary to the social order that characterize our public order, like Republic of Constitution and Law.

 In other words, the revival of the contradictions between the class interests of a society is the fundamental currency with which they work; promoting divisions and conflicts at all levels, in the family, at school, at work, in college, churches, etc.

Creating social organizations appearance of being independent of the Communists, is used to group people without ideological denomination, but with common interests to achieve certain claims of rights or ideas, this kind of organization usually recruited people with low educational levels and individuals close to committing crimes to solve their problems with social status.

However, the leadership of these organizations in the interests of those who created them, without their members never come to know that they are under the absolute control of the communist parties and the KGB.

You can see in the workers' unions and university students, at all levels, being under this control, highly efficient vector, to move them to the political positions that suit their brains´ controllers. As this domain is invisible, you cannot accuse these leaders to be acting on behalf of the enemy.

To create more confusion, Martin Luther King publicly was a Republican.

Was he, a Communist or a Religious Man?

By moving these strings behind the curtains, many of the ideas that are observed in the campaigns generated by the press, do not seem strange, such as the insistence on highlighting an uncontrolled budget for the country's defense. While this was heard in the US, the USSR, in the 60s, made a surprise plans to attack the US with nuclear missiles within a period not exceed 18 months.

That reality was not accessible to the international press, but quite the opposite. The press reacted by accepting the propaganda that painted socialism as a system of peace and international solidarity, world peace seeking to engage harmonic in developing the economy in the interests of human beings.

That idea of communism was reflected by the press. The campaign created internationally, through the Non-Aligned Countries, the International Committee for Peace, the Greens in West Germany, the Committee of the Nobel Prizes, to the International Human Rights Committee itself organizations were created and manipulated by Moscow and Havana for use as a seemingly spontaneous social organization, which agreed to support their interests, but without palpable direct connection with the USSR. To the International Human Rights Committee based in London itself, which served to advance the goals of the Soviet Union, were to change the balance of political forces during the Cold War. This created a backlash against the United States in countries where there were American military bases precisely to defend them from the attacks of the USSR. I remember seeing in Cuba, printed propaganda of the Greens, literature to oppose the use of Pershing's missiles in Germany that were made in Cuba.

Anti-war or peace movements seemed to be an independent force that arose spontaneously from the masses. Media supported them, and as such appeared in front pages of newspapers; but that spontaneity was "fabricated." Those who created the pockets of local military conflicts, with appearances of liberation movements, were the Soviets and Cubans to engage, in one way or another, with the United States; then increase these accusations of interference in the internal affairs of third countries. This "created" situation provided them to demonstrate the need to fight against "Yankee imperialism."

http://4.bp.blogspot.com/-_5mClG0aB6I/ULiNEadSpKI/AAAAAAAAAjs/Snl1q9hTGOA/s640/Bezmenov_subversion_chart_redrawn.jpghttp://4.bp.blogspot.com/-_5mClG0aB6I/ULiNEadSpKI/AAAAAAAAAjs/Snl1q9hTGOA/s640/Bezmenov_subversion_chart_redrawn .jpg

Chapter #15

The Subversive Campaigns

This is the general outline of the political subversion of the KGB against the United States during the period of the Cold War is an example to understand how it works and their coordination.

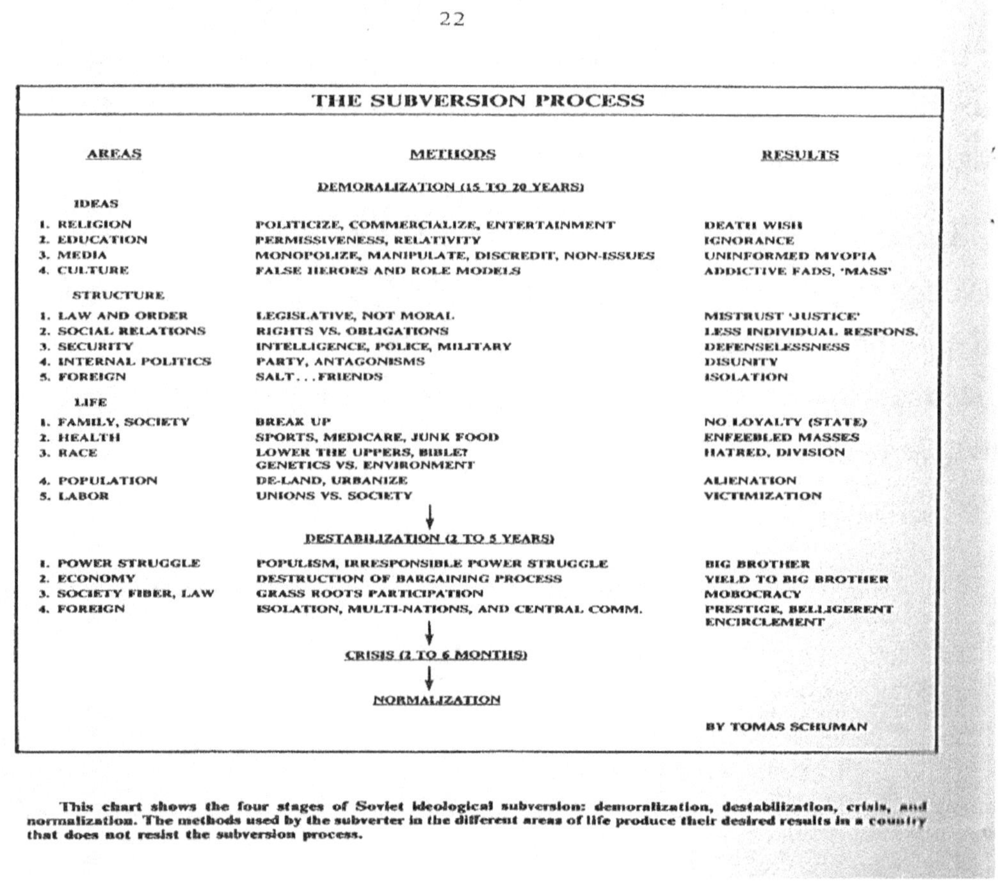

THE SUBVERSION PROCESS

AREAS	METHODS	RESULTS
DEMORALIZATION (15 TO 20 YEARS)		
IDEAS		
1. RELIGION	POLITICIZE, COMMERCIALIZE, ENTERTAINMENT	DEATH WISH
2. EDUCATION	PERMISSIVENESS, RELATIVITY	IGNORANCE
3. MEDIA	MONOPOLIZE, MANIPULATE, DISCREDIT, NON-ISSUES	UNINFORMED MYOPIA
4. CULTURE	FALSE HEROES AND ROLE MODELS	ADDICTIVE FADS, 'MASS'
STRUCTURE		
1. LAW AND ORDER	LEGISLATIVE, NOT MORAL	MISTRUST 'JUSTICE'
2. SOCIAL RELATIONS	RIGHTS VS. OBLIGATIONS	LESS INDIVIDUAL RESPONS.
3. SECURITY	INTELLIGENCE, POLICE, MILITARY	DEFENSELESSNESS
4. INTERNAL POLITICS	PARTY, ANTAGONISMS	DISUNITY
5. FOREIGN	SALT...FRIENDS	ISOLATION
LIFE		
1. FAMILY, SOCIETY	BREAK UP	NO LOYALTY (STATE)
2. HEALTH	SPORTS, MEDICARE, JUNK FOOD	ENFEEBLED MASSES
3. RACE	LOWER THE UPPERS, BIBLE? GENETICS VS. ENVIRONMENT	HATRED, DIVISION
4. POPULATION	DE-LAND, URBANIZE	ALIENATION
5. LABOR	UNIONS VS. SOCIETY	VICTIMIZATION
DESTABILIZATION (2 TO 5 YEARS)		
1. POWER STRUGGLE	POPULISM, IRRESPONSIBLE POWER STRUGGLE	BIG BROTHER
2. ECONOMY	DESTRUCTION OF BARGAINING PROCESS	YIELD TO BIG BROTHER
3. SOCIETY FIBER, LAW	GRASS ROOTS PARTICIPATION	MOBOCRACY
4. FOREIGN	ISOLATION, MULTI-NATIONS, AND CENTRAL COMM.	PRESTIGE, BELLIGERENT ENCIRCLEMENT

CRISIS (2 TO 6 MONTHS)

NORMALIZATION

BY TOMAS SCHUMAN

This chart shows the four stages of Soviet ideological subversion: demoralization, destabilization, crisis, and normalization. The methods used by the subverter in the different areas of life produce their desired results in a country that does not resist the subversion process.

In the mid-60s, more organizations appeared against the United States and to familiarize ourselves with the schemes that followed. The Russians allowed us to see what purpose they had and how they used the "useful idiots" to manage public opinion, which they called "state opinion. "As expected, the" state of mind. "Always favored them. The above examples were part of political subversion at that time, of which we still have many in memory.

After Operation "bridgehead," the KGB began a systematic action against the United States to subvert the social order and destroy the American nation. Let's look at the diagram illustrating the steps to achieve the complete destruction of a nation that has been targeted.

Remember that this process of social and political subversion is always under control, events or events that happen, as already mentioned, have no spontaneous character as they appear in the eyes of the beholder or ordinary citizen and everything is handled with the "active measures ",manipulated organizations and emerging leaders, who become more effective, as long as they win the support of the press.

The four stages of subversion political and ideological:

Demoralization

Destabilization

Crisis

Normalization

Demoralization is to operate a change in the perception of social and political phenomena prevailing in the environment where individuals from one country or geographical region operate. In other words, it is to create conditions for people to modify and develop attitudes or opinions contrary to those they had before.

When we are neutral, permissive or tolerant of all proposals of the enemy, we lose this battle; the enemy wins this battle very easily; Therefore, with this attitude, we do not conduct permanent and active opposition or input, and the enemy has expired. Neutral, is the number-one target of psychological warfare, to "prove," that there is corruption.

Communists can achieve the goal, in a period of about 15 to 20 years; simply exposing the ideology that professes the enemy to successive generations' frames destroying their moral and psychological reference. Points that exist outside the reach of the individual imagination, something that could be much better than what you know, creates motivational and cognitive stress, which we know as "Curiosity" in the city.

Recall that the "majority" rarely in history have had a leadership that actually represents a front to fight against minorities through repression, impose their reason to assimilate Leninism, which creates a Party, a small minority to draw the crowds at their convenience; Nazism did so, a minority dragged the German people to war. This happened in Japan with the Japanese militarists. This happens in all totalitarian countries when a minimum party leads and represses the clear majority, it is with Islamic extremists. A minority can kill and terrorize while a large majority of Muslim extremists may not be as their leaders.

Foster insecurity, through terrorism, economic chaos, unemployment, rising prices of items widely consumed by the induced scarcity, the real estate crisis, actively and deliberately create events to manipulate his interest.

<u>Just to mention some examples of demoralization we can cite: the hoist of the Mexican flag in the schools in California; the assassination of President Kennedy; establishing a cathedra of Marxist philosophy in an educational institution and create a fan association of Lenin or Che Guevara.</u>

Demoralization whose function begins to devalue, to disenchant the average citizen of the pillars supporting their society.

They undermine the prestige of an army by attacking a military garrison by surprise and then with the help of the press, exaggerate the defense response against the perpetrators of the fact as if they were tortured; make emerge an opposition leader denouncing alleged corruption or injustice and proposes new measures to amend problems that exist or may not exist, just to make people lose confidence in the institutions that should be pillars of the state.

Examples of ideological subversion in the United States used attack "Dark CIA and" Witch Hunter FBI "fake moon landings by NASA, publishing news coming out of the workshops of intelligence enemy agencies, or undermine the prestige of religion to the spread of information about the lewd activity of priests.

<u>In Cuba the assault on the Moncada's Barrack, was an example of demoralization against the Army of Cuba. The attack on JFK, hijacking of commercial aircraft, to shoot down Twin Towers, terrorist acts, manifestations of Women and Homosexuals are pure examples of demoralization.</u>

These examples are among the many ways to create, gradually neutralize concepts previously defended, or otherwise, which irritated and cursed us before<u>, we now see it without any reaction.</u>

 The core dragging society towards the enemy is made up of public misfits, nonconformists, the weak, pessimistic and enemies of personal sacrifice for the realization of themselves, psychopaths and sociopaths. These elements, enemy agents group them so that they give support to push their ideas using different institutions, which give them prestige and importance… as social figures.

This picture, in a few hours, was seen on social networks by a quarter of a million people, simply because they claimed that we were not born with racial preferences, however, the biological reality laid by our Creator, is that all species have a mechanism called specificity substrate consisting of hormones secreted by the penis into the uterus and carry a genetic code for the egg (ovule), appears from the body but has the same species, because in other ways they could cause random chaos, been created in the developed species. differently, these hormones, when they cannot produce adequate support, may cause uterine cancer. This is an example of the interests of the enemy by mixing the races using propaganda to increase interracial couples, this phenomenon, we have been a common factor where they want to plant subversive Marxist ideas by any means.

What results would they pursue with this monstrosity? It produces more conflicts in couples, families, and children, also changes the demographic structure of a nation and its cultural degeneration is rigged. As an example, when taking power in a nation like Cuba and Venezuela, it creates an artificial crisis in public services such as supplies of food, water, medical services, pharmaceuticals, energy, epidemics, etc.

With the help of the press, they characterize them as leaders, give legitimacy to expose the reasons for charging, will respect and strength; Therefore, more and more people join or are active in these groups.

 The KGB has used a pattern to select leaders based primarily on choosing those who are distinguished by their ability to lie and make promises, for his indolence and possessing a pathological egocentricity. This stage centralizes its activities in the areas of the economy, the family and the armed forces.

The history of these ideas were reborn in the thirties and after a decade of dalliance, the Frankfurt School is heading towards a new target, clean the discredited Marxism and all that is behind hangs like socialism, populism, fight class, the gulag, etc. using the same procedure but changing the language as it was known that the negative influence of the Bolshevik Revolution, its Lenin and Stalin had put them in a difficult situation of acceptance as a social system, because no people able to accept Marxism as a system, were positive, especially in Europe.

Trying to make a social engineering.

These ¨new¨ Marxists were looking for ways to revive the ideas of Marx, but with a different look for "a dynamic and important, working class." It could be handled without calling it a revolutionary class; then they came to graft on a dry tree of Karl Marx, a flourishing offshoot of the libidinous concepts of Austrian psychiatrist… Sigmund Freud.

This new "fruit" created to poison the man of Western culture, was the union of sex and politics. Since according to the Freudian conceptual scheme of personality in its three instances (the real self), is basically obsessed with sex impulses, (the id) and the frustrations created by the social norms of coexistence (social discipline, the superego or superego), this mixture is attributed to a Jew called Mark Horkheimer, who joined after Theodor Adorno and neo-psychoanalyst Erich Fromm, who argues that the differences between male and female are not aspects of some essential sex differences, but derive from differences in functions for life and have largely been set by society and not by nature, which it translates in practice too: ¨these differences are purely artificial, so being gay, is natural."

As we see, try natural or biological sex difference is as absurd as trying to cover the sun with one finger. Explaining does not seem necessary, biological differences function for all instances in all species of male and female in all its functions.

Herbert Marcuse joined the team, and attributed to exalt sex as the central element of the "Political Correctness", this graft became, in fact, the theoretical basis of the American left, thanks to the fabulous welcome that gave the Columbia University, in New York, directed by Nicholas Murray Butler and induced by Julián Gumperz and Willi Muezemberg, both KGB agents. (Communist Jews from the time of the Rosenberg spouses and more 30,000 of Soviet agents in the US).

American leftists´ current, was very attracted by the communist theories of openly criticizing society and the "American way of life," but have always kept silent about the violation of Human Rights and all the monstrous atrocities of Mao Tse Dong, Stalin, Castro, Ho Chi Min against their countries and the rest of the world.

The so-called Frankfurt School was an excellent "Trojan Horse," to continue with Marxist ideas the education. Laws were gaining ground, and today there is an impregnable bastion of Marxism at the in Congress, Senate, University of Berkeley, George Washington, Brandeis and Princeton, and in some way, we would say that the whole system of the US Education.

A black man and a white woman sitting apart symbolize the concept of social distance. Studies on social prejudices were used to neutralize the conservative concepts, theory Bogardus on the social distance appeared in the 40s by social psychologist's members of the Frankfurt School. .

The Social Distance is a measure of separation between social groups perceived or Caused by Differences Between groups of people as defined by well-known categories. It Manifests across a variety of social categories, including class, race and ethnicity, culture, nationality, religion, gender and sexuality, and age, Among Others. Sociologists Recognize three types of key social distance: affective, normative, and interactive.

They study it through a variety of research methods, ethnography and participant observation, Including, surveys, interviews, and daily route mapping, among other techniques.

Chapter 16

How to stop the Subversion?

Unfortunately, the only antidote against subversion is knowledge of the purpose and meaning of the enemy's plans for destruction, misery, and death. By not accepting neutrality, nor has any respect for the new rules-imposed cease to be neutral or indifferent. We need a Congress and Senate able to make Laws each one against the Eleven Points to fix every problem create until today.

The enemy knew how to stop the critical thinking of the mass. The anesthesia for each individual has a name, Political Correctness. This is the way to stop your Critic Thinking and your freedom of speech.

 They introduced the concept that just they can be use, the offending those around them, but they can express their ideas in front of You, and you need to be silent and approving others against You. Afraid to speak out, then sorry to think it. Express your ideas, be informed, get logic and clear argument to stop the enemies plan. If you are afraid to think it, then you will not express your idea, your traditional ideas, bored doing great for our Country, those ideas were corrected and necessaries, because the resulting were excellent and the better around the World. We need to get the Public Opinion in our side. Speak out your feeling anywhere and feel your Freedom in your pure and health reasons. God is with YOU and me.

Never accept ideas against your main ethical principle. at no time be neutral, when you re neutral, you are a loser! If you are silent, the enemy got your mind.

Remember, when we accept, we are putting our head on the block, so that the enemy can behead us. We must hold our pride with patriotic, democratic and religious values for new generations; explaining what they mean and ideas that expose the enemy; educating them not to be neutral or indifferent, creating harmonious and healthy personalities; teaching them to not have any respect for the ideas that they try to impose against the estate, inherited from the Fathers of the American homeland. Unfortunately, the only antidote against subversion is knowledge of the purpose and meaning of the enemy's plans for destruction, misery, and death. By not accepting neutrality, nor has any respect for the new rules imposed, WE, cease to be neutral or indifferent.

Brandishing educating patriotic values to recognize that much blood, so much heroism, sacrifice much, much pain cemented our society. We must create in our families, in our community, our environment a responsible attitude in every individual, not delegate any responsibility to the abstract collective or social level, because if we lose individual strength, now that you have read this chapter, we lose the war and our Freedom as you, and I, know "Freedom is not free."

In part, we need to change the way the Candidate showed his Plans. They must do a deep within coordination with the Social Psychology Department at the local College,   looking in the survey. What is the primary problem in the community with an open mind proposition? The college, and the high-school students may help in this job, like a political learning and expertise.

This resulting from this investigation will be public and then each candidate will show solutions for each problem. In the election, the winner will the compromise to fix the problem that everybody know we have. Until now, every candidate look for make a psychological impact to sell himself like a better product and get more money.

Annex 1

Soviet Intelligence Concepts: Active measures

Active measures (Russian: активные мероприятия) is a Soviet term for the actions of political warfare conducted by the Soviet (Cheka, OGPU, NKVD, KGB) to influence the course of world events, in addition to collecting intelligence and producing "politically correct" assessment of it. Active measures ranged "from media manipulations to special actions involving various degrees of violence." They were used both abroad and domestically. They included disinformation, propaganda, official counterfeiting documents, assassinations, and political repression, such as penetration into churches, and persecution of political dissidents.

Active measures included the establishment and support of international front organizations (e.g., the World Peace Council); foreign communists, socialist and opposition parties; wars of national liberation in the Third World; and underground, revolutionary, insurgency, criminal, and terrorist groups (1)

The intelligence agencies of Eastern Bloc states also contributed to the program, providing operatives and intelligence for assassinations and other types of covert operations.

Retired KGB Maj. Gen. Oleg Kalugin described active measures as "the heart and soul of Soviet intelligence": "Not intelligence collection, but subversion: active measures to weaken the West, to drive wedges in the Western community alliances of all sorts, particularly NATO, to sow discord among allies, to weaken the United States in the eyes of the people of Europe, Asia, Africa, Latin America, and thus to prepare ground in case the war really occurs."

Active measures were a system of special courses taught in the Andropov Institute of the KGB situated at SVR headquarters in Yasenevo, near Moscow. The head of the "active measures department" was Yuri Modin, former controller of the Cambridge Five Spy Ring.

Against the United States

A few claims of active measures against the United States were described in the Mitrokhin Archive: [1] Discrediting of the Central Intelligence Agency (CIA), using historian Philip Agee (code named PONT).

It attempts to discredit Martin Luther King, Jr. by placing publications portraying him as an "Uncle Tom" who was secretly receiving government subsidies.

Stirring up racial tensions in the United States by mailing bogus letters from the Ku Klux Klan, placing an explosive package in "the Negro section of New York" (operation PANDORA), and spreading conspiracy theories that the US government had planned Martin Luther King, Jr.'s assassination starting rumors that fluoridated drinking water was, in fact, a plot by the US government to affect population control.

Starting rumors that the moon landing was a hoax and the money ostensibly used by NASA was in actuality used by the CIA. Use of sympathetic elements in the press to name the strategic defense initiative as an impractical "star wars" scheme

Fabrication of the story that AIDS virus was manufactured by US scientists at Fort Detrick; the story was spread by Russian-born biologist Jakob Segal.

Not outside the context of the aggressiveness and historical irresponsibility displayed by the Soviet and Cuban rulers, is the crime committed against the United States, the assassination of President JFK. This crime becomes evident when discovering in the last years the reason why JFK was murdered and the Cubans and Soviets that participated in the organization and execution of the event, in American territory demonstrated with documents and photos where the participants with faces are identified and changed hair. This crime, as we all know, will mark forever the Contemporary History.

Nikita ordered Castro to kill JFK

The same characters who at some point later participated in the JFK

attack can be seen in the next picture, in May 1962, when Soviet

Prime Minister

Nikita Khrushchev threatens to destroy the United States if it attacks Cuba. Captain Emilio Aragones, who was the Nikolai Leonov to arrive in

the United States on August 23, 1963 with Aldo Margolles with intent to kill President J.F. Kennedy . Colonel Nikolai Leonov, who was in the Soviet embassy in the city of Mexico, November 22, 1963.

Nikita, Castro, Emilio Aragones, and Nikolai Leonov (behind Castro) in the Red Plaza of Moscow, presiding over the acts of May 1, 1962, the political objective of this act was to threaten the United States with a devastating blow.

The "Nomenklatura" of the USSR with Castro and Emilio Aragones in a forest... there was something very confidential to coordinate. Nikita S. Khrushchev, Nikolai Podgorny, Leonid Brezhnev, Nikolai Leonov, Fidel Castro and Emilio Aragones.

```
                                                    Date: 09/28/98
                                                    Page: 1

                 JFK ASSASSINATION SYSTEM
                    IDENTIFICATION FORM
...........................................................................
                    AGENCY INFORMATION

        AGENCY : CIA
 RECORD NUMBER : 104-10308-10144
 RECORD SERIES : JFK
AGENCY FILE NUMBER : 80T01357A
...........................................................................
                   DOCUMENT INFORMATION

    ORIGINATOR : CIA
          FROM :
            TO : UNOFFICIAL TO MR. ALFRED COX
         TITLE : ALDO PEDRO MARGOLLES Y DURNAL AND EMILIO ARAGONES Y NAVARRO PLOT TO
                 ASSASSINATE THE PRESIDENT OF THE UNITED STATES.
          DATE : 00/00/
         PAGES : 1
      SUBJECTS : MARGOLLES Y DUR
                 ARAGONES, EMILI
                 PLOT
                 ASSASSINATE
                 PRESIDENT
                 UNITED STATES

 DOCUMENT TYPE : PAPER, TEXTUAL DOCUMENT
CLASSIFICATION : UNCLASSIFIED
  RESTRICTIONS : OPEN IN FULL
CURRENT STATUS : OPEN
DATE OF LAST REVIEW : 09/19/98
OPENING CRITERIA :
      COMMENTS : JFK-WF02:F3 1998.09.19 11:55:02.513031:
```

The Soviet in control of Cuba's destiny. Colonel Leonid was saying goodbye one of the times that he went to IM [to break orders to the guerrillas in the Sierra Maestra in the year 1958. Emilio Aragones, evades the sarcastic gaze of the group, behind Alexei

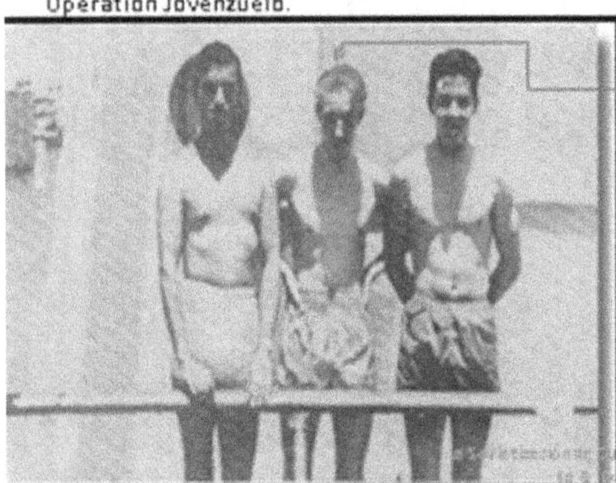

Victor Pina Cardoso, Alexei Leonov and Raul Castro returning from USSR 2 weeks before the Moncada assault, it action started the "Jovenzuelo Operation" ordered by Nikita Khrushev to Raul Castro in Moscu. The Operation planed kill 5,000 civil population, only 4 members knew the true KGB's Plan.

Victor Pina Cardoso, Nicolai Leonov and Raul Castro aboard an Italian steamer while returning from the USSR to Cuba, a few weeks prior to July 26, 1953. Leonov remained hidden in Menocal, Matanzas, Havana and Cayo Coco, Camaguey for many years as the operations officer in charge of Operation Jovenzuelo.

General KGB Nicolai Leonov
Second in Command of the KGB in 1989

Alexiev, Soviet ambassador to Cuba, Fidel Castro, the colonel of the KGB named by Nikita, Nikolai Leonov, a clandestine officer and advisor of the subversive Operation youngster since 1953 and Nikita Khrushchev... Everyone smiles by observing the chosen to execute JFK.

Declassified CIA document showing the names of Aldo P Margolles, Jose Llanausa Gobel, Emilio Aragones, Abelardo Colome, Raul Diaz Arguelles, Fabian Escalante, and Quintin Pino Machado as being part of the assassination of JFK captains Abelardo Colome

Ibarra and Emilio Aragones seconds before Oswald's shot in Dallas, November 22, 1963. Two of the 13 operatives of the Havana's Cuban Boys in United States territory to assassinate President JFK by order of Nikita. "Everything happens for a reason,"

Raúl Castro and Col. KGB Nicolai Leonov in the Sierra Cristal, 1958

After many years I managed to identify in a photo, perhaps taken without the intension that Abelardo Colome and Emilio Aragones were immortalized for history fulfilling this diabolical mission as all that fulfilled. At the time of overseeing the action of the attack on President JFK on November 22, 1963. General Colome left with 29 years of age, Emilio

Aragones thinner, with false hairs...

Both were at the pace of the caravan to ensure the execution of JFK. The man who watches JFK is evidently Emilio Aragones Deena's. Abelardo

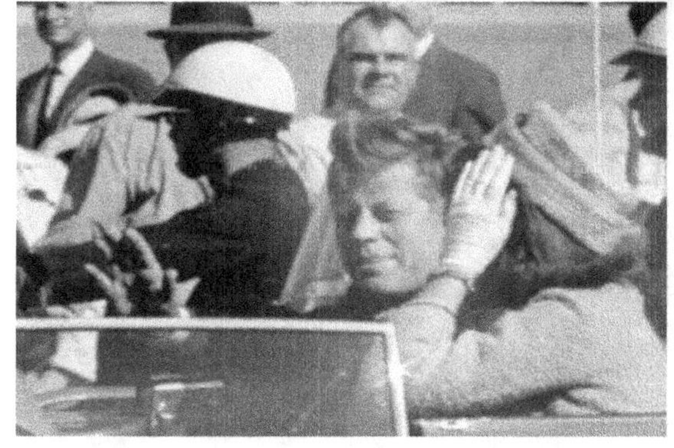

Colome Ibarra identified in the photo. The general Abelardo accumulation experience and merit to be general of Army Corps and to occupy the position of first Vice-minister of the Armed forces and head of the direction of the Control Organs (counter and military intelligence) for more than 25 years and after minister of Interior until his resignation. Jim Altegens AP Photos

Tens of Havana's Cuban Boys was in different cities of United States to coordinate with Jack Ruby and Lee Harvey Oswald the assassination of the President JFK. The

real story you can read in a book titled "The Havana Cuban Boys in Dallas"

Pictures composition and identification by the author. Ed Prida

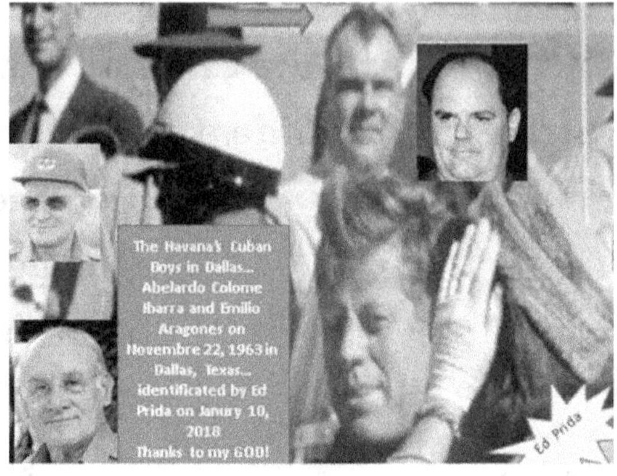

Jim Altegens AP Photos

Abelardo Colome, Aldo Margolles in the back of Emilio Aragones at 12:30 PM, Nov 22, 1963 in Dallas beside of JFK's motorcade, second before the Oswald shoots.

It seems that Castro sent a delegation to dismiss JFK and Nikita another delegation for a football game in honor of JFK, perhaps if we only have these photos anyone could present this elementary hypothesis. But hundreds of documents from the CIA, FBI, rent of houses, hotel accommodations, makeup, infiltrated Cuba in the CIA and four attacks on President JFK, it would not be easy to justify hi mong this group there are Viceministers of MinInt, officers with the rank of Commanders and a hierarchy of the Party like Emilio Aragonés, does not have many reasons to be of good will in the place of the fact. With these photos it seems that many conspiracy theories involving the CIA against President JFK, will not have much to explain ...
This is Commander Raúl Díaz Arguelles, behind Commander Abelardo Colomé Ibarra, Commander Aldo Margolles Dueñas and Captain Emilio Aragonés, National Coordinator of the ORI. In the group, an unidentified Soviet with a nose and glasses, his hair masked in black.

General Escalante insists on demonstrating that Antonio Veciana, Bernard Barker, José Ricardo Rabel, others were at the crime scene or in Dallas at this time, and it is true, they were in Dallas because they were agents of Cuba, not because the CIA had intention to kill JFK.

There were agents of the FBI, Police, Fire, CIA were fulfilling their functions within the territory of the United States. What is not causal and beyond the reasonable doubt is that the Cuban officers who entered American territory without legal documentation, were in link with Jack Ruby and Lee Harvey Oswald for months and then we found Victor Pina supervising the death of Lee Harvey Oswald inside the Dallas Police office.

Thanks for this strong affirmation. They even had rented houses in the name of the organization that founded Veciana, Alfa-66.

Nor does Eloy General Escalante remember that exactly at the time of Oswald's shot, his "Tavarich" from Minsk and Tampa, are the commanders Abelardo Colomé Ibarra, Raul Diaz Arguelles, Aldo Margolles and Captain Emilito Aragonés, accompanied by Lady Babuska, the Russian make-up artist, who put hair on Emilio Aragonés. You do not remember, neither from your false nose when leaving through the airport in Mexico.

The "Moscow-Havana's Boys in Mexico and Dallas"

Coronel KGB Nicolai Leonov
•Coronel Nikolai Leonov
•Coronel Oleg Nachiporenko
•Coronel Georgi Bolshakov
•Coronel Valery Kostikov
•Coronel Pavel Yatzov
•Coronel Yuri Montinsky

I could not miss Nicolai Leonov in all the fateful history related to the USSR and Cuba against the United States in the Soviet Embassy in Mexico on November 22, 1963 at the Soviet killer team played football in the backyard of the Soviet Embassy in the City from Mexico at 12:30 pm on November 22, 1963. Why were

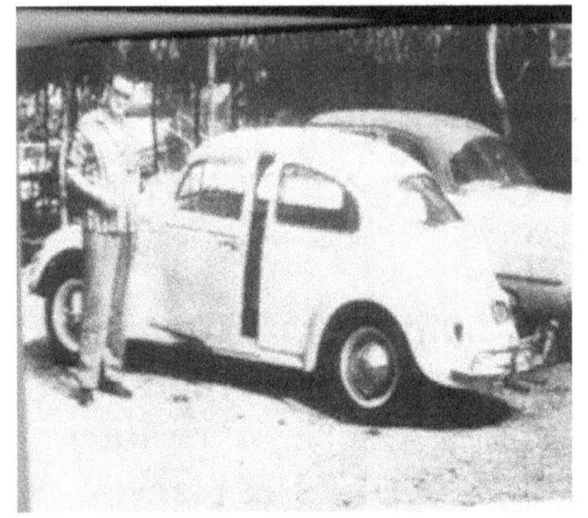

the KGB / GRU colonels of service in Washington and Havana playing soccer in Mexico City? They take the picture just at the time of the murder, check it with the position of the shadow of the midday sunlight. All happy, the Russians usually ake the serious photos 12:30 pm. presence as a simple tourist visit to see the President up close JFK.
 Many Cubans know that this yellow V VV car was owned by Captain Víctor Pina for many years, it was transported by an Antonov AN-12 from Cubana de Aviación to Mexico City.
Captain Pina drove this car until General Raúl Castro presented him with a 600 cc FIAT Polsky as a replacement in 1985. I drove this V W many times when Captain Pina visited my house in Rancho Boyeros.

Colonel Valery Kostikov of Section Z of the KGB, known as "kill 7". I was
waiting for the "news" on the Radio of the car on November 22, 1963 at 12:30
p.m. in Mexico City. Notice the shadow exactly at 12:00
Proof of them all knew what would happen in Dallas with JFK.

Supporting political movements

According to Stanislav Lunev, GRU alone spent more than $1 billion for the peace
movements against Vietnam War, which was a "hugely successful campaign and
well worth the cost.

Lunev claimed that "the GRU and the KGB helped to fund just about every antiwar
movement and organization in America and abroad.

According to General KGB Oleg Kalugin, said "Intelligence was unparalleled. ... The
KGB programs which would run all sorts of congresses, peace congresses, youth
congresses, festivals, women's movements, trade union movements, campaigns
against U.S. missiles in Europe, campaigns against neutron weapons, allegations
that AIDS... was invented by the CIA... all sorts of forgeries and faked material —
[were] targeted at politicians, the academic community, and the public at large".

Sergei Tretyakov, stated, "The KGB was responsible for creating the entire nuclear
winter story to stop the Pershing II missiles. Tretyakov says that the KGB wanted to
prevent the United States from deploying the missiles in Western Europe and that,
directed by Yuri Andropov, they used the Soviet Peace Committee, a government
organization, to organize and finance demonstrations in Europe against US bases.

He claims that misinformation based on a faked "doomsday report" by the Soviet
Academy of Sciences about the effects of nuclear war on climate was distributed to
peace groups, the environmental movement and the journal Ambio which carried a
key article on the topic in 1982.

Installing and undermining governments

After World War II Soviet security organizations played a key role in installing
puppet Communist governments in Eastern Europe, the People's Republic of China,

North Korea, and later Afghanistan. Their strategy included mass political repressions and establishment of subordinate secret services in all occupied countries

Some of the active measures were undertaken by the Soviet secret services against their own governments or Communist rulers. Russian historians Anton Antonov-Ovseenko and Eduard Radzinsky suggested that Joseph Stalin was killed by associates of NKVD chief Lavrentiy Beria, based on the interviews of a former Stalin's bodyguard and circumstantial evidence.

According to Yevgeniya Alabts allegations, Chief of the KGB Vladimir Semichastny was among the plotters against Nikita Khrushchev in 1964. KGB chairman Yuri Andropov reportedly struggled for power with Leonid Brezhnev.

Soviet coup attempt of 1991 against Mikhail Gorbachev was organized by KGB chairman Vladimir Kryuchkov. Gen. Viktor Barannikov, then the former State Security head, became one of the leaders of the uprising against Boris Yeltsin during Russian constitutional crisis of 1993.

Current Russian intelligence service SVR allegedly worked to undermine governments of former Soviet satellite states like Poland, Baltic states and Georgia, etc. During 2006, Georgian-Russian espionage controversy, several Russian GRU case officers were accused by Georgian authorities of preparations to commit sabotage and terrorist acts [citation needed].

Many NKVD agents were sent to join and penetrate the independence movements. Many puppet rebel forces were created by the NKVD and permitted to attack local Soviet authorities to gain credibility and exfiltrate senior NKVD agents to the West.

Political assassinations

The highest-ranking Soviet Bloc intelligence defector, Lt. Gen. Ion Mihai Pacepa claimed to have had a conversation with Nicolae Ceauşescu, who told him about "ten international leaders the Kremlin killed or tried to kill": Laszlo Rajk and Imre Nagy from Hungary; Lucreţiu Pătrăşcanu and Gheorghe Gheorghiu-Dej from Romania; Rudolf Slánský and Jan Masaryk from Czechoslovakia; the Shah of Iran;

Muhammad Zia-ul-Haq, President of Pakistan; Palmiro Togliatti from Italy; John F. Kennedy; and Mao Zedong.

Pacepa provided some other claims, such as a plot to kill Mao Zedong with the help of Lin Biao organized by the KGB and alleged that "among the leaders of Moscow's satellite intelligence services there was unanimous agreement that the KGB had been involved in the assassination of President Kennedy.

The second President of Afghanistan Hafizullah Amin was killed by KGB Alpha Group in Operation Storm-333. Presidents of the unrecognized Chechen Republic of Ichkeria organized by Chechen separatists including Dzhokhar Dudaev, Zelimkhan Yandarbiev, Aslan Maskhadov, and Abdul-Khalim Saidullaev were killed by FSB and affiliated forces.

Other widely publicized cases are murders of Russian communist Leon Trotsky and Bulgarian writer Georgi Markov.

There were also allegations that the KGB was behind the assassination attempt against the Pope John Paul II in 1981. The Italian Mitrokhin Commission, headed by Senator Paolo Guzzanti (Forza Italia), worked on the Mitrokhin Archives from 2003 to March 2006.

In a draft report, senator Guzzanti revived the "Bulgarian connection" theory concerning Mehmet Ali Agca's 1981 assassination attempt against the Pope John Paul II. Guzzanti declared that "beyond any reasonable doubt "the KGB was behind the assassination attempt against the Pope John Paul II in 1981

The commission draft report has no bearing on any judicial investigations, which have long been closed. The Italian draft report said Soviet military intelligence – and not the KGB – was responsible. In Russia, Foreign Intelligence Service spokesman Boris Labusov called the accusation "absurd."

The Italian Mitrokhin commission received criticism during and after its existence.[19] It was closed in March 2006 without any proof brought to its various controversial allegations, including the claim that Romano Prodi, former and current Prime minister of Italy and former President of the European Commission was the "KGB's man in Europe." One of the informers of Guzzanti, Mario Scaramella, has been arrested for defamation and arms trade by the end of 2006.

Guerrillas

Promotion of guerrilla organizations worldwide

Soviet secret services have been described as "the primary instructors of guerrillas worldwide According to Ion Mihail Pacepa, KGB General Aleksander Shakarovsky once said: "In today's world, when nuclear arms have made the military force obsolete, terrorism should become our main weapon." He also claimed that "Airplane hijacking is my own invention." In 1969 alone 82 planes were hijacked worldwide by the KGB-financed.

The Ernesto Guevara and Emilio Aragones in the Congo, Afrika. The Cuban Subversive Operation in the Black Continent for 35 years, millions of innocent persons deaths.

Lt. General Ion Mihai Pacepa described operation "SIG" ("Zionist Governments") that was devised in 1972, to turn the whole Islamic world against Israel and the United States. KGB chairman Yuri Andropov allegedly explained to Pacepa that a billion adversaries could inflict far greater damage on America than could a few million.

We needed to instill a Nazi-style hatred for the Jews throughout the Islamic world, and to turn this weapon of the emotions into a terrorist bloodbath against Israel and its main supporter, the United States.

The following liberation organizations have been allegedly established or supported by the KGB: Red Army Faction, PLO, National Liberation Army of Bolivia

(created in 1964 with help from Ernesto Che Guevara); the National Liberation Army of Colombia (created in 1965 with help from Cuba), Democratic Front for the Liberation of Palestine in 1969, and the Secret Army for Liberation of Armenia in 1975.

References and Sources:

PRISON THOUGHT: THE NATURE OF FUNDAMENTAL Political Correctness - http://tiny.cc/9bc08x
FRANKFURT SCHOOL 11 POINT PLAN - http://tiny.cc/9ec08x
BREITBART: TRANS UK PARLIAMENT REPORT - http://tiny.cc/gjc08x
Kalergi REFUGEES EUROPE PLAN - http:/Divide-and-ConquerOWARD PIVEN EUROPE - http://tiStratagem08x
YURI AND CULTURAL MARWatts RiotsNOV SUBVERSION - gradually/tiny.cc/muc08x
THE PAGES REVEAL Divide and Conquer MARXISM ' S INSIDIOUS MASTER Strategem - http://tiny.cc/zvc08x
Watts Riot California http://crdl.usg.edu/events/watts_riots/?Welcome
THE Hegelian Dialectic CONTROLLING AND ITS USE IN MODERN SOCIETY - http://tiny.cc/cxc08x
KGB DEFECTOR YURI BEZMENOV ' S WARNING TO AMERICA - http://tiny.cc/xrc08x
ZUR INSTITUTE: THE PSYCHOLOGY OF victimhood - http://tiny.cc/92s58x
LOOK FROM ABOVE: Hegelian Dialectic DEFINITION - http://tiny.cc/4au58x
THE APOSTLE OF THE LONG MARCH - http://tiny.cc/4su58x
Social Distance https://www.thoughtco.com/social-distance-3026589
General Reference:
Author Archives Bibliography:
http://www.fhu.com "Wake up and Save Your Country." The Foundation of Human Understanding. Roy Masters http://www.fhu.com/kgb-brainwashing-video.html No date. My transcript of a center portion, a 5-minute 8-second video interview excerpt of KGB defector, Yuri Bezmenov interviewed in 1984 by Edward G. Griffin. Transcript completed July 30, 2008, and posted on Newsvine.com. A longer interview was found on 7.2.09, 3.7.09 transcribed on, and proofed 07/04/09. Yuri Bezmenov interview, Longer version, 16.35, with French subtitles, uploaded 09/26/07: http://www.dailymotion.com/video/x32cxf_yuri-bezmenov Yuri Bezmenov, interviewé in 1985. Voir Aussi HTTP: // www.bafweb.com/2007/09/26/yuri-bezmennews idiots-utiles-du-socialism/ on HTTP: //www.dailymotion. com / video / x32cxf_yuri-bezmenov found July 2 , 2012 10:59 a.m. PDThttp: //larryh.newsvine.com/_news/2012/07/05/2998127-four-stages-in-subverting-a-nation-demoralization- destabilization-Crisis-normalization-his-thesis-leftists-are-the-useful-idiots-of-socialism- http://timesofthesigns.wordpress.com/2009/07/21/demoralization-destabilization/
https://www.yahoo.com/beauty/little-girl-has-perfect-answer-for-woman-who-wondered-why-she-wanted-a-doll-that-didnt-look-like-her-193253439.html
"Biohazard" Dr. Ken Alibek page 215
http://www.webster.edu/~woolflm/margaretmead.html
Yuri Bezmenov. Psychological Warfare Techniques. Conferences.
Woodroof Allport. The personality. Havana: Ediciones R, 1969.

Only operation. The FBI's man in the Kremlin John Barron. City: Regnery Publishing, 1995, pp. 59- 81; 87-96 and 112-115.

J Pete Earley. Camarade J . New York: Berkley Books, year?

Alexander Fursenko. One hell of the gamble. New York and London: WW Norton and Co., 19

Bibliography Consulted:

-Manual of Military Counter-Intelligence MINFAR, Cuba 1985

Yuri Bezmenov or Thomas Shuman Psychological Warfare conferences in Canada Techniques 7

-Personality by Woodruff Allport R Editions 1970 Cuba

Just operation. The FBI's man in the Kremlin John Barron Regnery Publishing pg 59-81 s 87-96, 112-115,

Comrade J Pete Earley New York edition Berkley Books

Alexander Furshenko "One hell of the gamble" ISBN 0-393-04070-4 WW Norton and Co. New York and London 1997

DAY Report About Soviet Advanced Military in Psychology 1972

Dr. Ken Alibek Biohazard by Dell Publishing Random House USA 2000

Documentary Film About Red Alert Cuba's Biological Weapons Program by Ed Palmer 1997 Miami, USA.

The Spy Who Saved the World by Jerold Schenker

Breaking With Moscow by Arkady Shevchenko

CIA Report About Maskirovka Means and Use by www.CIA.gov

Oleg Pentkosvsky The Spy Who Saved the World by Jerrold L. Schecter edition Charles Scribners's Sons New York, 1992

The Petrosky Paper by Oleg Pentkosky edition of Doubleday & Company New York 1965

Ronald Reagan 0123 Security Order for Security White House Washington DC the USA

http://www.newsmax.com/US/military-christians-chaplains-hostile/2015/04/16/id/638918/#ixzz3XYd8qHVv

http://freebeacon.com/national-security/russian-strategic-bombers-conduct-more-than-16-incursions-of-us-air-defense-zones/ By Bill Gertz - Washington Free Beacon - - Thursday, August 7, 2014

Author Archives and Testimonies

Conversations with my brother in law Barros Flight Engineer Rolando Guzman in 1946- 1971 Director and Chief of Operation of Cubana Airline

Conversations with Captain Victor Pina Cardoso, aka KGB Cor. Antonio Dahud and Eusebio López Azcué 1959-1990

Conversation with Captain Roberto Maqueira Counter Intelligence Officer Cuba 1964-1980

General Jose Abrantes Conversations with Ministry of Interior 1977-1990 Fernandez

Conversation with Captain Cesar Fonseca Alarcon 1958-1973 Chief of Pilots of Cubana Airline

Interview taped Commander Jaime Costa, member of 26th of July Movement, assault of Moncada Barrack and Granma invader. Rebel Chief of Army Intelligence Political Prisoner 1959 and after.

Conversation with US Navy Commander Harold Feeney (Quijote) DIA Chief of Intelligence Operation 1997-2002

09/26/07: http://www.dailymotion.com/video/x32cxf_yuri-bezmenov Yuri Bezmenov, I interviewé in 1985. Voir aussihttp://www.bafweb.com/2007/09/26/yuri-beNewsvineUseful Idiots-less-du socialism / on http://www.dailymotion.com/video/x32cxf_yuri-bezmenovfound July 2 , 2012

10:59 a.m. PDThttp: // larryh.newsvine.com/_news/2012/07 / 05/2998127-four-stages-in-subverting-a-nation-demoralization-destabilization-Crisis-normalization-his-thesis-leftists-are-the-useful-idiots-of-socialism- HTTP: //timesofthesigns.WordPress .com / 2009/07/21 / demoralization-destabilization /

https://www.yahoo.com/beauty/little-girl-has-perfect-answer-for-woman-who-wondered-why-she-wanted-a-doll-that-didnt-look-like-her-193253439.html

"Biohazard" Dr. Ken Alibek page 215

http://www.webster.edu/~woolflm/margaretmead.html

Bibliography:

1.-The Frankfurt School and its social influence Felipe Botaya, 2011

2. The tragic fate of Reason http://www.difusioncultural.uam.mx/revista/abr2005/palacio.pdf

3. Critical School of Frankfurt

Philosophical and sociological movement. Marxist philosophy. Max Horkheimer. Theodor Adorno. Herbert Marcuse. Rudolf Carnaphttp://apuntes.rincondelvago.com/escuela-critical-de-frankfurt.html

HIV epidemic, the most disastrous epidemic that has perhaps been

Psychological warfare operations against us and against you. Too.

Bibliography:

Author Archives

http://www.fhu.com "Wake up and Save Your Country." The Foundation of Human Understanding. Roy Masters http://www.fhu.com/kgb-brainwashing-video.html No date. My transcript of a center portion, a 5-minute 8-second video interview excerpt of KGB defector, Yuri Bezmenov interviewed in 1984 by Edward G. Griffin. Transcript completed July 30, 2008, and posted on Newsvine.com. A longer interview was found on 7.2.09, 3.7.09 transcribed on, and proofed 07/04/09. Yuri Bezmenov interview, Longer version, 16.35, with French subtitles, uploaded 09/26/07: http://www.dailymotion.com/video/x32cxf_yuri-bezmenov Yuri Bezmenov, interview in 1985. Voir Aussi HTTP: // www.bafweb.com/2007/09/26/yuri-bezmenov-les-idiots-utiles-du-socialisme/ on HTTP: //www.dailymotion. com / video / x32cxf_yuri-bezmenov found July 2 , 2012 10:59 a.m. PDThttp: //larryh.newsvine.com/_news/2012/07/05/2998127-four-stages-in-subverting-a-nation-demoralization- destabilization-Crisis-normalization-his-thesis-leftists-are-the-useful-idiots-of-socialism- http://timesofthesigns.wordpress.com/2009/07/21/demoralization-destabilization/

https://www.yahoo.com/beauty/little-girl-has-perfect-answer-for-woman-who-wondered-why-she-wanted-a-doll-that-didnt-look-like-her-193253439.html

"Biohazard" Dr. Ken Alibek page 215

http://www.webster.edu/~woolflm/margaretmead.html

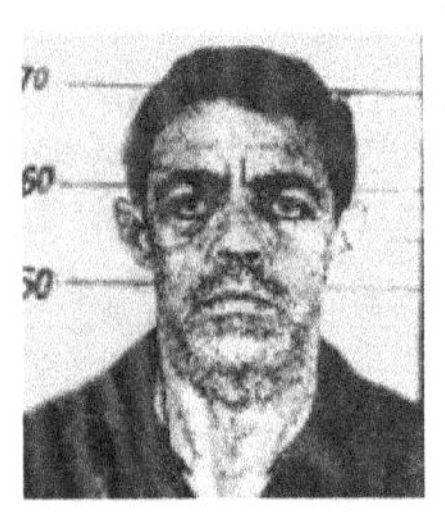 **Ed Prida Social, Forensic and Aeronautic Psychologist. Who worked as a Military Scientific Researcher and University Professor in the Minister of Interior and Air Force. Political Prisoner. Rescued from Castro's Prison by U.S. Rep Bill Richardson on Feb 11, 1996. Researches on Aviation, Psychology, Criminology and Political Intelligence. The Subversion against USA and Cuba", "The Sovietization of Cuba and its Consequences", "Raul's Delirium", "The Havana's Cuban Boys in Dallas", "The War in Angola", " Who did know Ernesto Guevara" "Actives Measures in Cuba", and others.**

Thanks to read the book. Your opinion will be Wellcome…my email es pridaissues@gmail.com

www.ingramcontent.com/pod-product-compliance
Lightning Source LLC
Chambersburg PA
CBHW081616250726
48657CB00009B/2592